Founded by Nina Grunfeld, Life Clubs are for anyone who wants to discover more about themselves, have space to think, or simply be happier.

These weekly workshops now take place around the country and are filled with like-minded people exchanging ideas, supporting each other and moving forward. In this book Nina provides you with some of the philosophies and tools of Life Clubs to work through in your own time. They may also inspire you to join a Life Club.

Contact Life Clubs on 0207 22 22 199 or www.lifeclubs.co.uk.

(Although some of the case histories in this book are loosely based on Life Clubs members, none of them will be recognisable. Everything that happens in Life Clubs is strictly confidential.)

the big book of us

nina grunfeld

✷ SHORT BOOKS

FIRST PUBLISHED IN 2007 BY

SHORT BOOKS

3A EXMOUTH HOUSE

PINE STREET

LONDON EC1R OJH

10 9 8 7 6 5 4 3 2 1

A CIP CATALOGUE RECORD FOR THIS BOOK IS AVAILABLE FROM THE BRITISH LIBRARY.

ISBN 978-1-904977-87-2

PRINTED IN THE UK BY BUTLER AND TANNER LTD, FROME & LONDON

DESIGNED BY TWO ASSOCIATES

To Michael, Frances, Ursula and Thomas and all their relationships – past, present and future

content

'If the stars
should appear but
one night every
thousand years
how man would
marvel and adore.'

Ralph Waldo Emerson

People don't usually have relationship training, and sometimes it shows.

You may have picked up this book because you're curious about how it can help you with your relationships. Well, it can. This book is written for anyone in a relationship, whether married, co-habiting or dating, straight or gay. To avoid confusion I have addressed the book to one member of the partnership but the exercises are designed for both partners to get involved in. One partner working through *The Big Book of Us* completely on their own can also get a lot out of it. So if you have a partner who doesn't want to join in initially, do some exercises yourself and then casually bring them into the conversation and see if you can gradually get your partner interested. For this book, the role of 'enthusiast' might just have to be yours.

Sometimes we get so used to our partners, we forget to look at them anew, as if we'd just met them. We forget to marvel and adore. This book will help you do that.

The Big Book of Us is structured to follow the natural flow of a relationship.

Chapter one

The chapter in which you learn relationship tools that you can use throughout the book – and throughout life.

Chapter two

This chapter is about you and your partner finding and appreciating yourselves, because you need to love yourself before you can love another.

Chapter three

The first meetings; those early times of attraction – 'Will we work together or won't we?'

Chapter four

The romantic chapter.

Chapter five

Not quite as romantic. Time to start thinking about your relationship and what it is all about. Maybe the cracks are beginning to show.

Chapter six

This chapter is for you and your partner as a team – working out how to compromise.

Chapter seven

Things may be getting a little rocky. This chapter will show you how to navigate through rows.

Chapter eight

You've got through the bad times – it's time to concentrate on the future.

The Big Book of Us **is about creating a successful relationship for you.**

Enjoying a successful relationship is about awareness. The more you become aware of yourself and of others, the happier you can be. *The Big Book of Us* is designed to make you become conscious of who you and your partner are and what you want. As you work through the book, answer the questions with total honesty or you won't learn anything about yourself – or your partner.

Take time to go through the book. There's no need to rush – an exercise a night (or even a week) is plenty. Savour working together and illuminating the contrasting parts of you and your relationship on different days. This book will help you understand the way you usually behave in a relationship.

Answering some of these questions may make you both become more vulnerable, so give each other lots of hugs, kisses and encouragement. The more difficult an exercise seems to you, the more essential it is; and, in this case, whilst there is more potential for growth, be aware that there will also be more potential for friction. *The Big Book of Us* is about creating successful relationships. But successful relationships aren't necessarily about being in agreement. Each of us brings our own views into a relationship and it's important that we acknowledge them – even if we don't agree with them. Being totally yourself makes a relationship fulfilling and creative. How do you feel about yourself – truly, deeply? What do you feel you deserve? If you don't believe you are worthy of a good relationship you'll put up with unacceptable behaviour. Lovers who put up with abuse – mental or physical – may believe that's all they are worthy of.

how it works

Each relationship you have will make you think differently about yourself and life. It will change you. Your partner's views will change you; as you affect each other, you grow together. This can be challenging or even frightening.

All relationships go through good and bad times, but it's the perspective you keep on your relationship that's important. If you see your relationship as bad, it'll take a lot to make it good, and conversely, if you see your relationship as good, it'll take a lot to make it bad. The more conscious and aware you become in your relationship, the more likely it is to be good.

What can destroy a relationship?
- **Arguing all the time**
- **No longer feeling close or connected**
- **Not feeling loved or appreciated**
- **No longer being friends**

The Big Book of Us will help to stop this negative spiral.

What keeps a relationship together?
- **Honouring and respecting each other**
- **Working on knowing each other**
- **Mutual understanding**
- **Appreciating each other's hopes and dreams**
- **Strengthening the friendship between you**

The Big Book of Us will help you do that.

Remember – the sum of you and your partner is greater than its separate parts. So get curious about what 'us' is all about. For most of the book you will be looking at your relationship, rather than at yourself and your partner as individuals – discovering what your relationship is, what it needs and where it is going. Once you know what your relationship wants, you can respond to it and let it grow.

How This Book Works

Your partner is referred to as 'they', rather than s/he.

Some exercises are to be done together and some are to be done separately by each of you in turn. In the latter case the exercise is repeated twice (usually on the following page so you can't see what your partner has written) and the word 'Partner ......' always appears at the top of the page, for you (or your partner) to write your name on the dotted line.

Take it in turns to be the first to fill in each exercise. 'Partner 1' and 'Partner 2' or 'Partner A' and 'Partner B' imply status. So fill in your name on the dotted line. Relationships are about equality.

There's lots of space for you to write in your book. Share it. Make it yours – a history of you and your partner together. Stick things in it, put dates on it – find mementoes (cinema tickets, bottle labels etc).

In most of the exercises you'll find an example or two – they are just there for guidance. Let them inspire you.

Work through from the beginning and take your time. If you want to be spontaneous and do any exercise that looks appropriate at the time – do it.

Be supportive of each other. Let your partner know how pleased you are to be doing this work on yourselves together. Praise them, listen to them, thank them, enjoy them.

These exercises are not designed for you to let rip at each other. They are for constructively working on your relationship. If at any stage you feel angry with each other, just stop and have a hug and a laugh, or take half an hour for time out. Do something completely different.

If you feel your relationship is as difficult as it was before you bought this book, seek professional help.

It takes courage to find out about yourself and your relationship. It takes courage to ask questions, to discover more about yourself. You'll feel fear, but also excitement. All relationships are about change – it happens whether we participate willingly or reluctantly, but the more conscious we are about the changes, the closer we'll become. We're looking for wholeness as a couple and yet every part of the relationship has its purpose – even the search and the struggle.

Here's to finding the light as well as enjoying the flame.

'Love must be as much
a light as it is a flame.'

Henry David Thoreau

1

useful **tools**

Your Tool Kit

As you go through this book, you'll find certain tools and ways of thinking will be used. There are five in particular to be aware of. The first, the Balance Chart, helps you to look at yourself and how satisfied you are with particular aspects of both your life and your relationship. It will also help you know what you want together for the future.

The next tool is about how to deal with a way of thinking called limiting beliefs. Limiting beliefs are those beliefs, not facts, we have that hold us back in our life – beliefs such as, 'I'm no good at relationships' or, 'I can't run very well'. The way we deal with them is the same each time, so it's a good idea to understand how to change them.

The third tool, feedback, is an essential tool for life in general. You are going to be working with someone very important to you and it's great to know how to give each other helpful and constructive feedback.

Personality typing, the fourth tool, isn't really a 'tool', but a recognition of how being different can be invaluable in relationships. This is a very brief introduction to personality typing and may just whet your appetite for finding out more about it. As you'll see, it's a great way to explore yourself and others.

Finally, apologies and compliments are included in this section because they are vital for any relationship and can be given all the time whilst working through *The Big Book of Us*. As usual, the more compliments (as long as they're truthful), the merrier.

Useful Tool 1: The Balance Chart

The Balance Chart is a visual representation of how you are feeling in your life at this moment in time. You're going to work with it in four ways.

1. **To see how satisfied you are with yourself and your life (i.e. as something separate from your relationship)**
2. **To see how satisfied you personally are with every aspect of your relationship**

3. **To work with your partner on how satisfied you both are with your relationship and to discover what you would both like to change**

4. **To affirm what you and your partner would each like for your future together**

Using the Balance Chart now

Start this book by filling out a Balance Chart twice, using different-coloured pens. Use the first colour when you go round the chart thinking about how you feel about yourself in each of the segments. Use the second colour pen to go round the chart again, this time working out how you feel about yourself *within this relationship.*

For example, in the Creativity segment you may feel good about yourself; you work in an area where there's a lot of problem solving and your brain is constantly being stretched. You also have photography as a hobby and your camera is always on the go. However, within the relationship you feel there's potential for stagnation. You tend to eat out at the same restaurants, see the same people and even make love the same way. So, you don't score yourself as highly in Creativity within the relationship.

This is the only time in the book that you are – or ideally, both of you are – going to fill out the Balance Chart for yourself. After this, you'll fill it out for your relationship – once at the end of the next chapter and once at the end of the book, so that you can see how much you've grown in your relationship as you've been working through the book. When working on your Balance Chart as a couple, bear in mind that you will probably have significant differences – use the Balance Chart as a starting point to working through them. Once you are aware of your differences, you'll be able to work towards a compromise.

Before you start

Read the introduction to each of the segments before you fill in your Balance Chart, so that you understand each of them fully. Then, just relax and go for it. Think about how you're feeling right now – and put a date on it so you can remember when you felt like this. This is only about today and what you want from your life and your relationship right now.

Circle 10 if you're feeling very satisfied with a segment and 1 if you're feeling very dissatisfied. Each time, circle the number that feels the most appropriate at this moment in time and then join up all the circles at the end for a snapshot of your life today.

Get curious

Once you have both completed your Balance Charts, talk about them with each other. Check out why you've scored yourselves in 3s and 4s rather than 8s and 9s (remember everyone has a different way of scoring themselves even if they feel the same way about something) and why, for example, you've scored yourselves particularly low in, say, 'Career' or 'Friends and Social Life', or whichever segment it is. Look at how you and your partner see your lives, both individually and together.

All part of you

Each segment of the Balance Chart is aimed at you assessing a different part of yourself. Make it your own. If you want to add a spoke, you can. You might find it difficult, for example, to think about your children and your parents under the blanket heading of 'Family', so add a 'Children' or a 'Parents' spoke. It's yours to have fun with. Add a 'Sex' spoke if this doesn't seem to fit into 'Love and Romance' – it's up to you.

Within each segment there are lots of things to think about. Here are some triggers to help you think as widely as possible about each segment, each time you go round:

Love and Romance
How satisfied am I with myself in this area of my life?

Do I feel loved and cherished? Do I love myself? Am I looking for love? Am I open to being loved? When was the last time I told someone that I loved them? Do I love enough? Am I aware of the importance of love in my life and in the life of others?

How satisfied am I with my relationship in this area?

Do I cherish the love in my life or do I take it for granted? Are there surprises in my love life – planned or spontaneous? Could we improve the love and romance in our relationship? What does love mean to each of us and do we like the ways the other expresses it? Is our sex life fulfilling? Do I like the ways my partner wants to make love and vice versa?

Home

How satisfied am I personally in this area of my life?

Is home a place of refuge from the outside world, a good place to return to? Does it warrant all the out-going costs and the work entailed in earning the money it takes to run it? Is it a place I would choose (now) or is it just the place I happen to live in? Does it feel as if it has a heart? Am I happy to be there on my own? What does the house say about me?

How satisfied am I with my relationship in this area of my life?

What does home mean for my partner and me? Are we in the right home for us? Do we share it successfully? Is it more mine than my partner's or vice versa? Is that OK? What could we do to make it more the way we want it? Does it reflect our values, intentions, creativity, taste and needs as a family, as a couple? Do we contribute equally towards making our home the way we want it to be?

Creativity

How satisfied am I in this area of my life?

What does creativity mean to me and how am I using it? When was the last time I was creative in relation to any difficulties I may be experiencing at home or at work? How does it make me feel when I have made something happen or created something – even a thought?

How satisfied am I with my relationship in this area?

What does creativity mean to us? Do we have creative outlets in our relationship? Are there situations in our lives in which we could be more creative at this moment?

thinking about me

'Our best thoughts
come from others.'

Ralph Waldo Emerson

Health and Fitness

How satisfied am I in this area of my life?

How do I feel about my general state of fitness and health? Do I honour my body? Am I aware of my body's language? Have I listened to it during the past week? Do I have health worries or niggles that I'm not acting upon? Am I quietly concerned with my health but don't know what to do? Do I have a good support system (dentist, osteopath, GP etc)?

How satisfied am I with my relationship in this area?

Is exercise a joint activity for us? If not, is that OK? How does health and fitness fit into the rest of our life? How important is it to us? When was the last time we took ourselves for a pleasurable walk or swimming or to the gym? Do I resent the amount of exercise you do or do not do, or vice versa?

Rest and Relaxation

How satisfied am I in this area of my life?

How rested did I feel when I woke up this morning? Do I wake up refreshed most days? How many hours of sleep do I generally need? And how many do I get? Do I rest when I know that is what I need? Do I know how to relax?

How satisfied am I with my relationship in this area?

Do we plan or make provision for relaxation in our busy life? Have we planned a holiday soon? Do we relax in the same way? Do we know how to relax as a couple?

Friends and Social Life

How satisfied am I in this area of my life?

Have I got the right balance between work and play? How often do I go out with my friends? When was the last time I spent some quality time with my friends? Are the friends in my address book the friends I want now? Do my friends drain me? Or do I feel valued by my friends? Can I share with them? Do I ever wonder what friendships are all about?

How satisfied am I with my relationship in this area of my life?
How is our social life panning out this week? Who takes the lead in planning our social life? Is that OK? Do we support each other socially – how could we support each other better? Which friends energise us as a couple and which drain us? Do we share all our friendships, or see some friends on our own? Do either of us feel jealous of the other's friends? Have I dropped friends I'd still like to see because my partner didn't like them or vice versa?

Career
If you don't have a conventional career, use this segment to reflect on what you mainly do with your time. Running a household can be a full-time job in itself. There may be community projects or voluntary work you're involved in.

How satisfied am I in this area of my life?
How does my career fit in with other aspects of my Balance Chart? Am I fulfilled in my work? Do I have unresolved work issues? Do I put up with abuse at work because of my financial needs? How does my work relate to my core values? Am I realising my full potential at work? What would I like to achieve? What work do I dream of doing?

How satisfied am I with my relationship in this area?
What does my career bring to our relationship? And what does it take away? What does my partner's career bring to our relationship and what does it take away? What boundaries would I like my partner to set around their career? What would I like my partner to achieve? What would we like to achieve as a couple?

Family

This does not have to refer to a conventional 'family unit', it could refer to the community you live in, or to extended family.

How satisfied am I in this area of my life?

Am I making time to be with my family? Are they aware of my needs and where I'm coming from? Do I have any grudges I need to clear/deal with? Am I coping with the demands of my family? What do I get from my family and what do they get from me?

How satisfied am I with my relationship in this area of my life?

Are our families uniting us or pulling us apart? Are they part of our life together? When was the last really memorable and happy day we spent with our families? Do we feel that we are always giving to our families or do we receive from them as well?

Money

How satisfied am I in this area of my life?

Is my financial situation working for me and to plan? Do I have a plan? Do I use my money creatively and wisely? Does my money serve me well? Do I have problems with money or attitudes that get in the way of earning and honouring money? Does money control me or do I control it?

How satisfied am I with my relationship in this area?

Do we both have the same views about money? What do we want money for as a couple? Does money represent power in our relationship? How satisfied are we with our financial set-up and the way in which we employ money? Who deals with our money? Do I earn more than my partner (or vice versa) and is this a problem? Do I spend more than my partner (or vice versa) and does this matter? What could we do to ensure that we aren't worried about money?

Balance Chart next page

Spirituality

How satisfied am I in this area of my life?

Am I aware of my spiritual needs and whether I have any? If I wish to meditate or pray, am I able to find time to in my life? If I belong to groups or religious organisations are they working for me? Am I at peace with myself and the world? Am I dealing with my very human need to find meaning in what I am doing? Do I trust my inner self, and wisdom?

How satisfied am I with my relationship in this area of my life?

If we believe different things, does it matter? Do we feel we belong to anybody or anything, or even to each other? Are we aware of how we are growing and changing all the time? Do either of us feel jealous of or excluded by the other's spirituality?

My Balance Chart

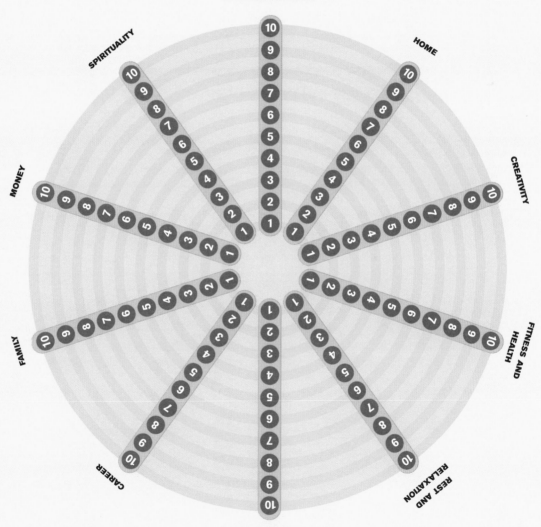

My Balance Chart/2

Partner ....   Today's date ....

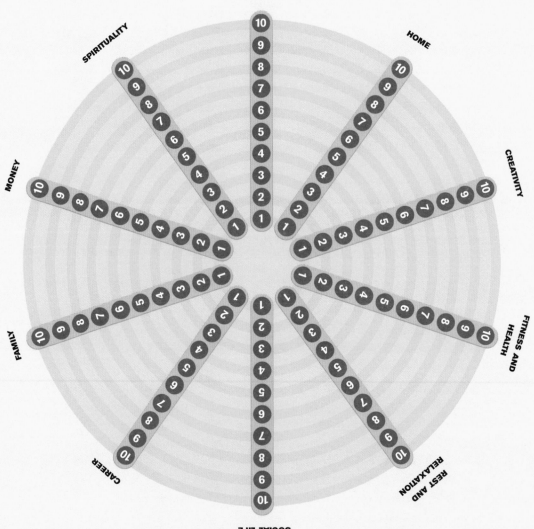

Useful Tool 2: Understanding Limiting Beliefs

Colin's mother left home when he was four. He grew up with a father who could no longer trust women and never remarried. What's more, his father always made derogatory remarks about his mother – and women in general. Colin came to believe that all women left their partners sooner or later. So when he started dating, rather than relaxing and allowing himself to fall in love and build a relationship, he tended to be difficult and unpleasant right from the start. As well as behaving aggressively he would challenge these women for hours into the night, questioning them over and over again about how much they loved him. Needless to say each of the women he has been involved with has left him early on in the relationship. This has meant that Colin can prove himself right: all women are bound to run away and it will be impossible for him ever to have a long-term partner.

Amanda, on the other hand, was told by her stepfather from an early age that she was too independent, and not the kind of girl a man would want to marry. Attractive, vivacious and, of course, highly independent, she has never been out of a relationship, but none of them has lasted for longer than a year. She has destroyed her relationships to prove her stepfather right.

Both Colin and Amanda are hampered by what are known as limiting beliefs – negative beliefs (albeit very different ones) about their ability to have a long-term, loving relationship. In Colin's case he has to start believing that not all women run away and Amanda has to let go of the idea that her father was always right, and believe that many men like (and want) independent women.

Many of us have adopted negative beliefs about our ability to have good relationships. We can easily believe that we're 'the kind of person' who has 'those kinds of relationships'. It feels comfortable, convenient even, to think in terms of stereotypes: 'I always fall for men who boss me about', 'None of the women I long for will ever commit to me' or even, 'All the men I like are married'. Yet if you look at your beliefs dispassionately you will see that, if you think like that, you will meet men who'll boss you around, or independent women or married men. You've set up a limiting belief about your ability to meet someone different – someone with whom you're going to be able to have a loving, fulfilling relationship and until you get rid of these limiting beliefs you won't be able to move on.

Getting rid of limiting beliefs

There are several stages to getting rid of your limiting beliefs and it's important to think about the stages as you see them here – in a logical progression. Start by identifying your limiting belief. Become aware of how much this belief is holding you back and then think about how your life would change if you altered your way of thinking (usually to the opposite of what you believe at present). Then think about all the reasons, hidden or otherwise, you might have that make you want to stay in your comfort zone with this limiting belief.

Let's think about Colin and his limiting belief that women are going to run away from him. What advantages does Colin get from this belief? When women leave Colin, apart from proving him right, he has the opportunity to mess around and meet a lot more women. It also stops him from having to risk being hurt as he always destroys the relationships before he gets too involved; so he doesn't really have to expose himself emotionally to these women. By being with each of them for such a short time he can keep his feelings private. So there are lots of 'good' things for Colin about destroying these relationships.

Once Colin becomes aware of these advantages, he is able to decide to do something about them. He begins to realise that it would be good to have someone to share his life with. He can decide that he'd like to open up to a woman and take the risk of being hurt, that he wants to commit himself and share his time with someone else. Colin realises that his ideas about women are simply excuses, and yet, it is still difficult to give up the myth of the unfaithful woman.

Once you have become aware of the reasons *why* you are limiting yourself, you can decide whether you want to stay in the same place in your life, or if you could perhaps find the same 'comfort' elsewhere – from doing or thinking other things.

One At A Time

There's space on the next two pages for you and your partner to each work on one of your limiting beliefs – although you can always work on more using a sheet of paper. Be really honest with yourself – otherwise you won't achieve anything. There's an example given below to show you how it works – note the present tense.

Partner ....

My existing limiting belief

(eg I don't trust anyone)

....

What two – three advantages do I lose by getting rid of my limiting belief?

(eg I lose the feeling of being in control, I lose being allowed to be private, I lose only having myself to blame if things go wrong)

....

What three actions can I commit to that will help get rid of my limiting beliefs?

(eg I can start sharing secrets and being more open, I can trust that things will be alright even when I'm not in control)

....

If I take one of these actions, when and where am I going to do it and how many times this week am I going to do it?

(eg I'm going to commit to reserving Wednesday night for seeing friends – and invite the first one now)

....

My new belief

(eg I am more trusting of others)

....

What 2-3 things are possible with this new belief?

(eg I can allow myself to feel more loved, I am more outgoing and less lonely, I have greater self-esteem)

....

One At A Time/2

Partner ....

My existing limiting belief

(eg I don't trust anyone)

What two – three advantages do I lose by getting rid of my limiting belief?

(eg I lose the feeling of being in control, I lose being allowed to be private, I lose only having myself to blame if things go wrong)

What three actions can I commit to that will help get rid of my limiting beliefs?

(eg I can start sharing secrets and being more open, I can trust that things will be alright even when I'm not in control)

If I take one of these actions, when and where am I going to do it and how many times this week am I going to do it?

(eg I'm going to commit to reserving Wednesday night for seeing friends – and invite the first one now)

My new belief

(eg I am more trusting of others)

What 2-3 things are possible with this new belief?

(eg I can allow myself to feel more loved, I am more outgoing and less lonely, I have greater self-esteem)

Useful Tool 3: Giving Feedback

You're going to be giving each other a lot of feedback as you work through this book, and it's essential to give it sensitively. Whether you just want to get something off your chest or let your partner know where they stand, you need to be as tactful as you can be.

Ted and Sheila have to share their home office, which is a difficult situation for Sheila as Ted is very untidy. The issue of tidiness has come up between them before, but has never been satisfactorily resolved. One day Sheila decides to take a different tack. Instead of being exasperated, she starts with a positive comment, 'I really enjoy working in the same room as you – your creativity is inspiring.' Needless to say, this puts Ted in a receptive mood for hearing what else Sheila has to say. She then gets him further involved by asking him a few questions in the hope that he'll come to the same conclusion as her: 'How are you finding things, Ted? What would you like to change or improve about our work space?'

Because Sheila has involved Ted, he is now interested in hearing her ideas. Instead of attacking him with, 'I find your clutter really annoying', which she normally does, Sheila phrases her feedback so that it is based on facts and emotion rather than criticism: 'I'm finding it difficult to work in a space where I feel overwhelmed by the clutter.' For the first time, Ted is able to listen to how upset Sheila is by his untidiness. He agrees to take action – and does. Sheila has managed to communicate the direct and negative impact that Ted's clutter has been having on her, without turning it into a personal attack on him.

This positive way of giving negative feedback is a very useful tool when working in a partnership. Feedback needn't be unpleasant – it's an essential part of communication and, when given appropriately, can be tremendously constructive. We all want to know how others perceive us, and how our actions affect them. Feedback helps us know where we stand in our relationship and keeps it on the right track. Like compliments, keep the positive feedback going when working through this book.

'The only man I know who behaves sensibly is my tailor; he takes my measurements anew each time he sees me. The rest go on with their old measurements and expect me to fit them.'

George Bernard Shaw

Useful Tool 4: Personality Typing

There isn't space in this book for an entire section on personality typing, but it's something to start becoming aware of – namely that each of us looks at the world through a different lens.

It's easy to see what we all have in common – the need to be loved, the desire to leave our mark, a need for meaning. Yet we all approach life in different ways and this can be bewildering. Think about your partner, your family members, your colleagues, your friends. Every single one of them is different and sees life differently, which is very confusing. If we all behave differently, how can we predict what another person will do? And, just because we want something, it doesn't always follow that our partner will want it too.

If you can understand where someone is coming from, it is easier to work with them and realise that their actions are not an attack on you, but stem from themselves.

A little quiz

Let's start by thinking about this simple scenario to introduce you to one facet of your personality type. You're at a party – either all sitting around the table or standing up and mingling. How do you behave? Choose the option below that seems most like you.

1. **Do you do whatever you can to help: pass food around, gather up plates – even do the washing up?**
2. **Do you find someone you like the look of and talk to them all night? It could be the person sitting next to you at the dinner table or just someone at the party**
3. **Do you mingle and talk to as many people as you can, keeping an eye out for anyone who looks interesting and prefer a general conversation at the dinner table, rather than being monopolised by one particular person?**

By answering this question, you will have started thinking about where you get your energy from.

answers over

If you answered 1 You are a 'hunter-gatherer' type. You've got an inbuilt need to survive. You'll probably enjoy shopping, have a full fridge, collect books, video games, antiques (or anything else) and be in control of your finances.

If you answered 2 You get your energy from one-to-one conversations, from intimacy and from a perpetual searching for someone to bond with. You're a 'one-to-one' type who craves intense relationships – even eye contact energises you.

If you answered 3 You're the 'group' type and you get your energy from being part of a group. You either are with a group or you're thinking about how you relate to groups (and you might not always feel as if you do). And, as your focus is on groups and therefore society, this means that manners are very important to you – you see them as oiling the wheels.

Each of us gets our energy in these three ways, but we all have one way that we favour, that we use more often than the other ways and one way that doesn't suit us as much. So, you might be a 'one-to-one' person who loves intense conversations, but can't cope with family parties with too many groups of people to talk to and so you become a 'hunter-gatherer' and start handing round food.

   Knowing you're a 'group' type might make sense of why you find it essential that people say 'Please' and 'Thank you' and help you with laying or clearing the table. It might also explain why your partner gets upset if you keep the fridge bare – they're a 'hunter-gatherer' type and you're a 'group' type and just not interested in shopping for food. So let them shop and cook if that's what they enjoy. As a 'group' type you're happy to eat whatever's going – preferably in the company of friends or family. It's people that are important, not food. Similarly, if your partner wants to talk to you through the night and you just want to go to sleep, it may be that they're a 'one-to-one' and you're not. Give them some complimentary feedback and drop off to sleep.

   Be aware of your differences and enjoy them. By being conscious of them you'll rub along a lot easier.

Useful Tool 5: Apologies And Compliments

Many of us find it difficult to say sorry and admit that we made a mistake. But letting your partner know that you've been thinking about the issue and have realised that you stepped out of line, or that you have said something you've regretted and are prepared to apologise, is an enormous compliment to them and breaks down barriers quicker than almost anything else. Don't let pride or stubbornness stand in the way of apologising. If you feel you've done something wrong, just say so.

It may seem strange to include compliments in useful tools, but you're going to be doing a lot of soul-searching whilst going through this book and you'll want to feel loved and appreciated by your partner, as they'll want to feel loved by you.

You know how good it feels when someone says, 'Well done' or, 'You look great' or, 'You handled that so brilliantly'. People whose self-worth is low sometimes can't take in compliments. If that's the case with you, don't worry: you'll be working on yourself over the next few chapters and will start to enjoy getting compliments.

Compliments are the oil in our relationships. We all need to be appreciated, to feel loved and admired and special. If you don't honestly enjoy complimenting the person in your life, think again about your relationship. Otherwise telling someone they did something well (no matter how small) is a wonderful thing to do and can give you almost as much satisfaction as the receiver of the compliment.

If you're not used to being complimentary about each other, start now. Practice really does make perfect. Notice how you're making your partner feel as you say something nice to them. And, above all, be honest. What's the betting they'll soon say something nice to you too?

Useful Tools is all about...   using the Balance Chart
working through limiting beliefs
giving constructive feedback
learning to apologise
enjoying compliments

two halves make a whole

2

me+me = us

How Do I Feel About Myself?

Before you can have a loving, committed relationship, it's important to feel good about yourself. The way people feel about you is a mirror of the way you feel and until you know just how much you're worth, you can't expect anyone else to. You'll also find that each relationship challenges the way you think about yourself, so it's best to start by having a good self-knowledge and by feeling comfortable in your own skin.

Liking yourself consists of being able to look after every aspect of yourself and helping yourself grow and reveal yourself to the world. It's about becoming aware of who you are – and how wonderful you are.

Fiona was a pupil at a high-achieving school. From an early age she was told (and believed) she had to be the best at everything. In her forties, Fiona was highly successful in her chosen field as a banker, but found she couldn't form a lasting relationship. Her deep-seated belief that she had to be the best didn't allow her the time to invest in anything other than her career. And whenever she got involved in a relationship, she had to be the best in that too. She just didn't know how to relax, enjoy being herself and being with someone else – everything with Fiona was about doing.

Once Fiona started working on herself, she began appreciating herself and everything she was – even when she didn't try. By focusing on her natural strengths, Fiona realised that she could afford to slow down and make time for herself and a relationship.

Start by thinking about who you are and what you bring into a relationship and then we'll start working on how you can love yourself even more.

Who I Am

Complete the three sentences below as fast as you can. Just blurt, without any modesty – false or otherwise. You may find the negative side of yourself easier to access at present, but by answering these questions you'll begin to realise just how much you've got going for you.

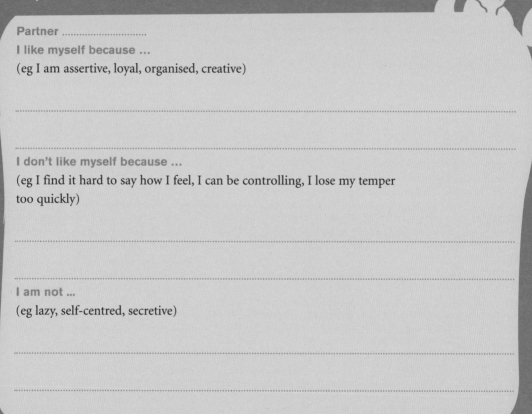

Partner ....

I like myself because ...

(eg I am assertive, loyal, organised, creative)

....

....

I don't like myself because ...

(eg I find it hard to say how I feel, I can be controlling, I lose my temper too quickly)

....

....

I am not ...

(eg lazy, self-centred, secretive)

....

....

Who I Am/2

Partner ....

I like myself because ...

(eg I am assertive, loyal, organised, creative)

I don't like myself because ...

(eg I find it hard to say how I feel, I can be controlling, I lose my temper too quickly)

I am not ...

(eg lazy, self-centred, secretive)

'To love oneself is
the beginning of a
life-long romance.'

Oscar Wilde

Love Yourself First

Debby didn't really rate herself, and every time she got a compliment from anyone (friend, colleague or partner), she'd start questioning the intelligence or the honesty of that person. 'Why are they so complimentary about me?' she used to ask. 'If they rate me, how can I take them seriously?' And, one by one, she destroyed her relationships because of her lack of love for herself. After a while Debby realised that something was up. Why was she the only one among her friends who was still single? She started working on herself and slowly began to blossom.

Nearly all of us have a side that can't quite believe people we admire could possibly admire us in return. And yet the more secure we feel in our love for ourselves the more we will be able to believe it. No relationship can work without you believing that someone is as lucky to have you as you are to have them.

Having a good relationship with yourself is the firmest foundation for any relationship with someone else. Think about how wonderful you are to your friends and give yourself the same treatment. First, get to know yourself. Begin to understand what you enjoy doing on your own. Spend a day (or an hour a day) just doing what you want – and notice what you like. Where do you relax best – on the phone, reading a book, listening to some good music or playing a game of tennis? Do more of it. What makes you laugh most – a funny film, a group of friends or going to watch a stand-up comic? Do more of that too. Make a date with yourself. Splash out. Where will you go and what will you do? What compliments really make your day? Give some to yourself and, while you're at it, why not make a list of all the compliments you've ever been given, and just enjoy getting them all over again.

Imagine You Are Your Own Best Friend

Answer the eight questions below, circling the relevant number between
1 and 10 (10 for loving a great deal and 1 for not loving much at all).
If you noticed you scored less for loving and looking after yourself than
you did for loving and looking after your best friend, think of ways you
could appreciate yourself a little more.

Partner ....

How much do I love my best friend?   1   2   3   4   5   6   7   8   9   10

How much do I love myself?   1   2   3   4   5   6   7   8   9   10

How much do I support and look after my best friend?   1   2   3   4   5   6   7   8   9   10

How much do I support and look after myself?   1   2   3   4   5   6   7   8   9   10

How much do I prioritise my best friend's needs?   1   2   3   4   5   6   7   8   9   10

How much do I prioritise my own needs?   1   2   3   4   5   6   7   8   9   10

Examples of how you could show your appreciation of yourself:

- **By asking for what you want**
- **By giving yourself more time for you**
- **By not putting yourself down**
- **By eating healthy, nurturing, nutritious food**
- **By loving yourself as well as others**
- **By complimenting yourself**

**Think about what would work for you, what you would really like to do
for yourself, and write it down.**

Imagine You Are Your Own Best Friend/2

Partner ....

How much do I love my best friend?　**1　2　3　4　5　6　7　8　9　10**

How much do I love myself?　**1　2　3　4　5　6　7　8　9　10**

How much do I support and look after my best friend?　**1　2　3　4　5　6　7　8　9　10**

How much do I support and look after myself?　**1　2　3　4　5　6　7　8　9　10**

How much do I prioritise my best friend's needs?　**1　2　3　4　5　6　7　8　9　10**

How much do I prioritise my own needs?　**1　2　3　4　5　6　7　8　9　10**

Examples of how you could show your appreciation of yourself:

- **By asking for what you want**
- **By giving yourself more time for you**
- **By not putting yourself down**
- **By eating healthy, nurturing, nutritious food**
- **By loving yourself as well as others**
- **By complimenting yourself**

Think about what would work for you, what you would really like to do for yourself, and write it down.

Protect Yourself

Now you've begun thinking about yourself and how you deserve to be looked after and cared for, the next step is actually doing it. No matter what anyone says, self-love is not the same as being selfish. You're not going to look after yourself any more than you already look after everyone else. Self-love doesn't stop you caring for others, it makes it easier for you to do so – and it reminds you to focus on yourself as well.

You have to nurture yourself. Just as a jug pouring water for many people has to be refilled, your energy reserves have to be replenished otherwise they will run out and you will be of no use to anyone – least of all yourself.

Anna is a busy mother with an office at home. One day a group of clients from out of town came to see her. When they arrived the weather was fine, but when they left after a lengthy meeting it was raining. Anna's immediate instinct was to offer to take them to the station, but she was exhausted from the meeting and it was only a short time before she would have to transform herself into mother mode and cope with the demands of her children, their school day and their homework. With that in mind she decided against taking them to the station. She didn't even lend them an umbrella. And, of course, they didn't ask for one. After all, they could take care of themselves. By putting herself first she had more time to recover her energy and more time to give to her family. She'd made the right decision for her.

who influenced me?

Saying 'No'

Some people find it enormously difficult to say 'No'. In a relationship, especially if you are the type of person who wants to please, you can end up agreeing to do all sorts of things that you don't feel like doing. You might end up enjoying something you never thought you would. But you might also end up unhappy or exhausted or both.

Self-knowledge can move you on enormously in life, so listen to your intuition and if it tells you what you truly want and that includes saying 'No' to someone or something, just do it. Be your own best friend, value yourself and take care of yourself. Remember that saying 'No' to others is often saying 'Yes' to yourself.

A good relationship makes allowances and compromises so that both partners can be honest about what they want and where their boundaries lie.

How I Became Me

Each of us has been influenced by the other relationships we have had in our lives and by the key people we've met along the way. Maybe your father taught you to say 'No', or maybe it was your first love who made you aware that the simple pleasures (like a picnic in the park or a bicycle ride) were the most fun; a teacher at school may have introduced you to another culture and showed you that life could be lived in a different way or perhaps a sibling took you to rock concerts and gave you your first taste of freedom. Go through your relationships over the decades and think about who you were influenced by; who were the significant people in your life and what impact they had on your thoughts on relationships and on life.

Partner ....

Decade	Influential people	How they influenced me
0-10		
10-20		
20-30		
30-40		
40-50		
and on ...		

How I Became Me/2

Partner ....

Decade	Influential people	How they influenced me
0-10		
10-20		
20-30		
30-40		
40-50		
and on ...		

Gaining In Confidence

Looking back over previous relationships will have helped you to see where your confidence – or lack of confidence – has come from. Now it's time to work on changing any under-confident feelings you may have, because we can all improve our confidence in ourselves. We may be frightened to change our feelings – it's often more comfortable to stay as we are. But once we realise how limiting comfort can be, we can move on. Boosting your self-confidence will help you to take on new challenges in your life. Start now by thinking of a phrase that feels difficult for you to say (for example, 'I'm a great lover' or 'I look fabulous') and say it over and over again to yourself. Simply repeating a simple phrase – maybe each time you look in the mirror – will help you believe in yourself. Think how you use praise to encourage others and praise yourself.

As you work through the following quizzes on pages 55 and 56, you'll notice the similarity with limiting beliefs (page 29). Once you know what you find comforting about being under-confident, you can challenge it. So, let's think of ways to help your confidence grow, because once you believe in you, you'll realise your partner already believes in you – you just couldn't see it.

Five ways to start becoming confident:

1. Focus on what you can do – what you already feel confident about doing
2. Work out the supposed 'advantages' to being under-confident – then you can challenge them
3. Give yourself credit for everything you do (that's why we note achievements every week at Life Clubs). Everything you attempt will feed your confidence
4. Don't put yourself down – instead of saying, 'I'm quite good at tennis' or, 'I'm OK at organising', say 'I enjoy tennis', 'I'm good at organising – I can handle that for you'
5. Set yourself simple, manageable goals all the time – things you've been putting off doing, things you didn't think you could do. Watch your confidence grow as you achieve those goals

Confident People

- Trust in their own abilities
- Take control of their lives
- Accept compliments graciously
- Think positively
- Trust in their own abilities
- Accept themselves as they are

go for it

'If you hear a voice within you say "you cannot paint," then make sure you paint, and that voice will be silenced.'

Vincent Van Gogh

Confidence Quiz

Write down an under-confident feeling that you have. It could be about you in a relationship. Once you have understood this line of questioning, you can use it to work on any of your feelings of under-confidence.

Partner ....

What is my existing lack of self-confidence?
(eg I'm embarrassed about my body)

What is my new feeling of confidence?
(eg I feel very comfortable in my body)

What advantages would I get from having this new attitude? (at least three)
(eg I would be able to make love with the light on, I would feel more adventurous sexually, I would feel more attractive, I would become more confident)

What advantages are there to staying as I am? (at least three)
(eg I feel safe, I can get sex over and done with quickly, I can hide, I can remain passive)

What excuses do I make as to why I don't change? (at least three)
(eg I don't want to have sex, I'm shy and I don't want people to notice me, I'm tired and I need my sleep at night)

What three actions could I commit to that would help get rid of my lack of self-confidence and help me to gain my new feeling of confidence?
(eg I could tell myself I look beautiful until I believe it, I could believe my partner when they tell me I am beautiful, I could start exercising)

Take one of those actions: when are you going to do it and where are you going to do it?

Confidence Quiz/2

Partner ....

What is my existing lack of self-confidence?
(eg I'm embarrassed about my body)

What is my new feeling of confidence?
(eg I feel very comfortable in my body)

What advantages would I get from having this new attitude? (at least three)
(eg I would be able to make love with the light on, I would feel more adventurous sexually, I would feel more attractive, I would become more confident)

What advantages are there to staying as I am? (at least three)
(eg I feel safe, I can get sex over and done with quickly, I can hide, I can remain passive)

What excuses do I make as to why I don't change? (at least three)
(eg I don't want to have sex, I'm shy and I don't want people to notice me, I'm tired and I need my sleep at night)

What three actions could I commit to that would help get rid of my lack of self-confidence and help me to gain my new feeling of confidence?
(eg I could tell myself I look beautiful until I believe it, I could believe my partner when they tell me I am beautiful, I could start exercising)

Take one of those actions: when are you going to do it and where are you going to do it?

Looking Good

As you saw in the confidence quiz, your self-image can be a major issue. Self-image relates to most aspects of your life. It leads naturally into relationships, because if you're feeling unattractive you may not want to be touched by a partner or you might feel inhibited sexually. There may even be a stage before this, because if you aren't feeling attractive it can mean you're not open to having a relationship. How you feel about your outer image naturally has an effect on how you feel about your inner self, and your personality.

We've all had enough debates about who is beautiful to know that beauty is most definitely in the eye of the beholder. What's stopping you from seeing yourself as beautiful? How often do you see people you consider to be beautiful or handsome who themselves aren't aware of their powers and slink into the room almost apologising for their presence? Similarly we have all seen people who we wouldn't say were conventionally beautiful but who emanate self-confidence and are attractive and charismatic because they glow from top to toe. Their self-image is very positive. They don't worry about what others think of them, they know they are beautiful – and they are right.

But what makes one shine from within? I'd like you to think about what you could do to achieve that inner confidence. On the following pages there are a few tips – no doubt you can think of a few of your own.

looking even better

How To Achieve That Inner Glow

Physical

- First thing in the morning, whilst still in bed, stretch ten times and then drink a glass of water – your first of eight
- Breathe deeply – breathing rhythmically and deeply will help you regain your energy and stay calm
- Hot and cold showers – have a cold shower after a hot one to close your pores and invigorate you
- Make sure you smell good – wash thoroughly and use cologne or perfume to lift your spirits

Mental

- Think about what you want to achieve to give your life purpose and direction
- Exercise your brain – absorb new things, enjoy working through this book, do brain teasers
- Be grateful – become aware of everything you have in your life, including your body
- Keep challenging yourself – become aware of your fears and conquer them one at a time
- Believe in yourself

A little effort

- Find your own style and take the trouble to look good – even if you're not seeing anyone, it's important for you
- Find the good points of your physique and accentuate them
- Be straight – stand and sit up straight
- Get enough sleep – use cat naps if necessary
- Eat consciously – eat slowly and as healthily as possible

Thinking of others

- Do some work for other people – giving makes you feel good
- Listen to others closely – that's real communication – and learn from them
- Laugh often – find friends to laugh with and watch comedies on TV
- Enjoy yourself and others will enjoy you

'We are what we
repeatedly do.
Excellence, then,
is a habit.'

Socrates

Act As If

Act as if you are excellent – as Socrates says – and you will begin to feel excellent.

- If your self-image is that you are fat, you will overeat and not exercise
- If your self-image is that you are you are a drunk, you will drink to excess.
- If your self-image is that you are a loser, you will act like a loser
- If your self-image is that you are depressed, you will act in a depressed way

But …

- If your self-image is that you are intelligent, you will confidently solve problems and make decisions
- If your self-image is that you are friendly, you will be easy to get to know, sociable and outgoing
- If your self-image is that you are handsome/beautiful, you will pay close attention to your physical self and appearance, and know you are attractive
- If your self-image is that you are a winner, you'll act like a winner

Thinking Positive

It's time to think about you in the context of relationships. You've had good relationships that you can learn from and it's worthwhile remembering them because they are the key to the kind of relationships you like and value, and to who you become in a relationship.

Begin by making a list of all the good relationships you've ever had – including the ones you are currently in. Think about the relationships that brought out the best in you, the relationships in which you felt fulfilled and the relationships in which you felt you grew as a person. These don't just have to be romantic, they can be any relationship with friends and family.

Include people with whom you can be yourself and relaxed. Those who make you feel safe and secure. Once you know what works for you, you'll know what to look for in a romantic partner.

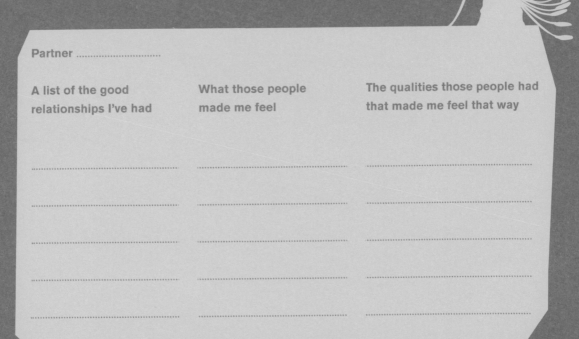

Partner ....

A list of the good relationships I've had	What those people made me feel	The qualities those people had that made me feel that way
....	....	....
....	....	....
....	....	....
....	....	....
....	....	....

Thinking Positive/2

Partner ....

A list of the good relationships I've had	What those people made me feel	The qualities those people had that made me feel that way
....	....	....
....	....	....
....	....	....
....	....	....
....	....	....

My Core Values

In this chapter we've been thinking about how it's a good idea to get to know yourself before you can get to know someone else. Your values are key to who you are. They are the views you have taken on as you have grown up, and are still important in the way you live your life, no matter what else changes. Nothing is as important as finding someone who shares your core values – sharing hobbies or interests isn't as vital to the wellbeing of your relationship as sharing the same values.

One of John's values was dependability and so, when he and David were invited out to a last-minute party with some exciting new friends, he apologised and said that the two of them had an earlier prior engagement. David, on the other hand, was not big on dependability. He was livid, said he would rather have gone out with the new friends and cancelled the boring couple they'd invited to dinner. The values of John and David were in conflict and it led to disagreement.

Of course your values can change through experience or meeting people you admire. You may find that some of your values are obsolete or stand in the way of your happiness and so you'll want to get rid of them. You may also want to adopt new ones – maybe some to share with your partner to help you in your future together. David could become more dependable and notice how upsetting his flippancy can be, and John could bring a little bit more spontaneity into their lives.

Think together about how your respective sets of values make you feel about these key relationship issues:

- Money
- Children
- Making decisions
- Honesty and fidelity
- What divorce means to you
- Obligations to others
- The future

finding my values

'Only the man who crosses the river at night knows the value of the light of day.'

Chinese proverb

Discovering My Values

See if you can identify some of your values by using these simple exercises. Each time you come up with an answer, ask yourself, 'What was important to me about *that*?' Then, with that answer, ask the same question again, 'What was important to me about *that*?' and so on, until you come up with the value.

Partner ....

Think about a peak experience

(eg watching the sun go down on holiday, giving birth, running a marathon)

....

What was it about that experience that was important to you?

....

Get curious about what you'd do if you were boss for the day

(eg scrap rules, give everyone the day off, make all staff work overtime)

....

Why would it be important to you to do that?

....

What would you do if you won the lottery?

(eg give it all to charity, take a cruise, invest it all and carry on as before)

....

Why would it be important to you to do that?

....

Describe your ideal day

(eg take the children swimming, go hang-gliding, lie in bed reading)

....

What is it about your ideal day that is important to you?

....

Discovering My Values/2

Partner ....

Think about a peak experience

(eg watching the sun go down on holiday, giving birth, running a marathon)

....

What was it about that experience that was important to you?

....

Get curious about what you'd do if you were boss for the day

(eg scrap rules, give everyone the day off, make all staff work overtime)

....

Why would it be important to you to do that?

....

What would you do if you won the lottery?

(eg give it all to charity, take a cruise, invest it all and carry on as before)

....

Why would it be important to you to do that?

....

Describe your ideal day

(eg take the children swimming, go hang-gliding, lie in bed reading)

....

What is it about your ideal day that is important to you?

....

Ideal Relationships

We've been thinking about the 'me', now it's time to think about the 'us'. Twice in this book you're going to go through the Balance Chart with your partner planning what you want from your relationship, your home, your life and your time together. Just relax and enjoy it.

1. Look at the Balance Chart on your own and write down what you want in an ideal relationship from each segment. Write it in the present tense and in the positive. There is a page for each of you on which to write down all of your fantasies – big or small. Write down as many things as you can think of.

   eg Love and Romance
   In my ideal relationship we buy each other random little gifts to show our love for each other
   eg Home
   In my ideal relationship I have space in my home for myself
   eg Creativity
   In my ideal relationship we make a window every week to have a brainstorming session about what we want to do that week

2. Then ask your partner to do the same without looking at your ideas.

3. Next give each of your partner's ideas a mark out of 10 for how important they are to you. '10' is for very important, '1' is for not so important. Those ideas you've given between 7 and 10 to are the ones to think about bringing into your relationship now if you can. They are the most important ones for both of you – and likewise the ideas of yours that your partner has given between 7 and 10. Where you don't agree, you can start thinking about compromise.

4. Together, go round the Balance Chart to show how successful you think you are being right now in creating your ideal relationship – mark each area in turn. If you don't agree, just split the difference and circle a compromise number. Work out what you both want to do next week to start changing things.

If your partner can't, or doesn't want to, take part, do the Balance Chart on your own to see how successful you think you are both being right now in creating your ideal relationship.

what we could have

'Tread softly
because you tread
on my dreams.'

William Butler Yeats

Dreams For Our Future

Partner ....
Segments of Balance Chart

Partner ....
**How important is this
idea of your partner's
for you (mark out of 10)**

Love and Romance In my ideal relationship …

....

Home In my ideal relationship …

....

Family In my ideal relationship …

....

Creativity In my ideal relationship …

....

Health and Fitness In my ideal relationship …

....

Rest and Relaxation In my ideal relationship …

....

Friends and Social Life In my ideal relationship …

....

Career In my ideal relationship …

....

Money In my ideal relationship …

....

Spirituality In my ideal relationship …

....

Dreams For Our Future/2

Partner ....
Segments of Balance Chart

Partner ....
**How important is this
idea of your partner's
for you** (mark out of 10)

Love and Romance In my ideal relationship …

Home In my ideal relationship …

Family In my ideal relationship …

Creativity In my ideal relationship …

Health and Fitness In my ideal relationship …

Rest and Relaxation In my ideal relationship …

Friends and Social Life In my ideal relationship …

Career In my ideal relationship …

Money In my ideal relationship …

Spirituality In my ideal relationship …

Our Balance Chart

Today's date ....

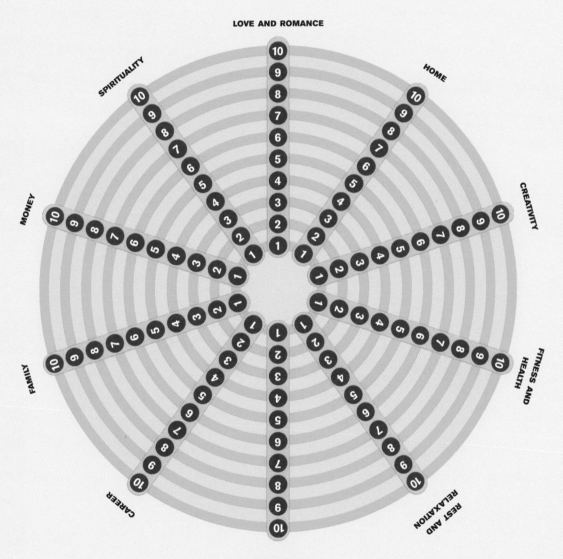

'Love does not consist of gazing at each other, but in looking together in the same direction.'

Antoine de Saint-Exupery

Me + Me = Us is all about ...   finding out what I like about myself

loving myself first

thinking about how I love myself compared to
   how I love my best friend

understanding how to become confident

realising that thinking positively will help
   change me

learning to protect myself

learning to say 'No' when I want to

wondering who influenced me

analysing what I like in my relationships

discovering my values

working out what we want

liking us

3
liking us

Being Good At Us

You have now worked through two chapters of *The Big Book of Us* and it's time to think about you and your partner together, as a unit. This chapter is unashamedly romantic. It's an exploration of what you love about each other now and what you loved about each other when you first met.

Answering these questions will also help you find out about yourself. What makes you feel romantic? What stops you from being this loving all the time? What do you value most about yourself in this relationship? And what do you value most about your partner?

Share your warmest thoughts. It can be difficult if you're used to taking your partner for granted or are worried that you may be rejected, but just think how it will make you both feel.

It's also time to think about how you are together physically. When was the last time you felt a frisson as you brushed past your partner? When was the last time you held hands? When was the last time you kissed? The more physical contact you give each other the more you'll feel like having. Start hugging your partner now and notice how good it feels.

Why not start sharing sexual thoughts and fantasies too? Talk to each other about what turns you on and what you'd like more of. Ask them what they'd like to try but are a little bit afraid of – and tell them what you'd like to try too. In the spirit of romance, check that your bedroom is as welcoming as it could be, make love there – or anywhere else – regularly. Act romantic and you'll feel romantic.

So Happy Together

Relax and enjoy the following few pages. Ideally, you and your partner will each answer the quiz in turn, and then share your thoughts. However, if you are doing this alone, there is still much to be gained from filling out the quiz. Be as honest with yourself as you can, and then return to reflect on your answers at a later date. You will surprise yourself.

Partner ....

What do I get from my partner that I enjoy the most?

When our relationship is good, how do I feel towards my partner?

When do I feel most like a loving partner?

What are the ways my partner has made a difference to my life?

What are the ways I think my partner would say I've made a difference to their life?

What in my life is better than I ever thought it would be?

What do I want more of?

What will keep us together?

So Happy Together/2

Partner ....

What do I get from my partner that I enjoy the most?

....

When our relationship is good, how do I feel towards my partner?

....

When do I feel most like a loving partner?

....

What are the ways my partner has made a difference to my life?

....

What are the ways I think my partner would say I've made a difference to their life?

....

What in my life is better than I ever thought it would be?

....

What do I want more of?

....

What will keep us together?

....

Our Diary

Start a diary today. Just keep it for a week. In it record how things have been between you and your partner that day. If you enjoy writing this diary perhaps you will keep it going.

Think positive. It's too easy to notice each other's faults and flaws. Write down any and every pleasure that your partner has given you. Did they pick up their dirty clothes from the bedroom floor or put their wet towel back in the bathroom? Did they surprise you with a bunch of flowers? Or did you remember a happy holiday abroad you spent together and decide to cook something exotic you shared there? Did your partner pay you a compliment? Did you experiment making love? Have you been able to resolve any problems you might have?

the best thing was...

Our Diary

Monday   **Date** ....

Partner ....   Partner ....

What was the best thing that happened today between you and your partner?

....

....

....

....

What did you do to improve your relationship today?

....

....

....

What did your partner do to improve your relationship today?

....

....

....

Our Diary

Tuesday   **Date** ....

Partner ....   **Partner** ....

What was the best thing that happened today between you and your partner?

....

....

....

....

What did you do to improve your relationship today?

....

....

....

....

What did your partner do to improve your relationship today?

....

....

....

....

Our Diary

Wednesday   **Date** ....

Partner ....   Partner ....

What was the best thing that happened today between you and your partner?

....

....

....

....

What did you do to improve your relationship today?

....

....

....

....

What did your partner do to improve your relationship today?

....

....

....

....

'After all these years, I see that I was mistaken about Eve in the beginning; it is better to live outside the Garden with her than inside it without her.'

Mark Twain

Our Diary

Thursday   **Date** ....

Partner ....   Partner ....

What was the best thing that happened today between you and your partner?

....

....

....

....

What did you do to improve your relationship today?

....

....

....

....

What did your partner do to improve your relationship today?

....

....

....

....

Our Diary

Friday   **Date** ....

Partner ....   **Partner** ....

What was the best thing that happened today between you and your partner?

....

....

....

....

What did you do to improve your relationship today?

....

....

....

....

What did your partner do to improve your relationship today?

....

....

....

....

Our Diary

Saturday   **Date** ....

Partner ....   **Partner** ....

What was the best thing that happened today between you and your partner?

....

....

....

....

What did you do to improve your relationship today?

....

....

....

....

What did your partner do to improve your relationship today?

....

....

....

....

Our Diary

Sunday   **Date** ....

Partner ....   Partner ....

What was the best thing that happened today between you and your partner?

....

....

....

....

What did you do to improve your relationship today?

....

....

....

....

What did your partner do to improve your relationship today?

....

....

....

....

I Fell For ...

Once you've taken stock of your present feelings, go back and explore how you felt in the past about each other. Thinking about your early feelings will strengthen the bond you have with each other now. Cast your mind back to how you felt when you first met. There may have been something that attracted you to your partner from the first second – or maybe there wasn't, but you grew on each other. Sometimes it can be difficult to articulate what it was like when the passion first kicked in or how it hit you when you first fell in love.

The way you feel goes much deeper than words. It hits you in your heart. Passion is not only about what you see in a person as they stand in front of you or with their arm around your waist. It's also to do with feelings – perhaps long buried – and your fantasies and vision for your future together, even if that future is not yet defined.

It's time to reconnect with those first feelings. Here's a quiz for each of you – a memory quiz. Remembering those early thoughts and fantasies will bring a little romance back into your life.

All Over Again ...

Pretend you've just met and start exploring your emotions. Write down as
many things as you can think of. When you've both completed the quizzes,
share your thoughts and acknowledge each other's honesty.

Partner ....

What attracted me to you?
(eg your intelligence, your nervousness, your hair, your body)

....

....

What do I think attracted you to me?
(eg my vagueness, my shoes, my hands, my bike)

....

....

What brought us together?
(eg our sporting prowess, our humour, our bicycles, our love of the cinema)

....

....

What was the first occasion when I knew I'd fallen for you?

....

....

What was my vision for our future?
(eg we'd emigrate together, we'd work together, we'd have a family together,
we'd always be so attracted to each other)

....

'Did my heart love till now? Forswear it, sight, for I ne'er saw true beauty till this night.'

William Shakespeare

All Over Again .../2

Partner ....

What attracted me to you?
(eg your intelligence, your nervousness, your hair, your body)

....

....

What do I think attracted you to me?
(eg my vagueness, my shoes, my hands, my bike)

....

....

What brought us together?
(eg our sporting prowess, our humour, our bicycles, our love of the
cinema)

....

....

What was the first occasion when I knew I'd fallen for you?

....

....

What was my vision for our future?
(eg we'd emigrate together, we'd work together, we'd have a family
together, we'd always be so attracted to each other)

....

Whole Lotta Love

This is an exercise to work on together. Fill the heart with everything you love about each other. You could write in it, stick bits of favourite song lyrics in it, stick in a photo or two, even some hair. Make it *your* heart.

Liking Us is all about ...   appreciating each other
remembering how we met
thinking back to our early attraction
sharing our heart

let's explore

4

curious us

'If we could see
the miracle of
a single flower
clearly, our whole
life would change.'

Buddha

Assumptions

Now you have reconnected with how loving you feel towards each other, it's time to get curious again. In amongst those 'What attracted us to each other …' questions that you've just answered (see pages 89-91), you may well realise that, at the time, you made some assumptions about who your partner was, and you may well be making some about who your partner is now. It's easy to make assumptions, but this chapter is about staying open, curious and adaptable. About assuming you know nothing about the other. About wanting to learn everything about them. Because, for a relationship to grow, you can't take anything for granted.

Where do our assumptions come from?

- Our family/upbringing
- Our core values
- Our culture
- Formative experiences
- Our education – at school, church, university
- Relationship experiences to date
- Personal hang-ups/insecurities
- Our fantasies

We make most of our assumptions without even being aware that we're making them. How many times have you been to a party, met someone and pigeon-holed them with a particular job (eg a doctor) because of something they were wearing, only to discover that they were something quite different (eg an artist)? How do you feel when you realise that you have made a completely wrong assumption?

How can our assumptions mislead us? They can …

- Reflect and reinforce our prejudices
- Influence our assessment of others – especially on the first encounter
- Lead us to misjudge people/situations
- Close us off from forming relationships with new people
- Limit our experiences and perspective
- Make us become complacent/stuck in a rut
- Prevent us from growing/developing as people

Often we make the assumption that our partner will continue to do what they've always done. But that is not always the case.

Mary was anticipating her 50th birthday with trepidation. She did not know how to celebrate it and assumed her partner was waiting for her to make the arrangements. In over twenty years of marriage she had always planned the parties so she was amazed and delighted when her partner arranged a surprise party. Mary's assumption that her partner would make no plans to celebrate her milestone birthday were turned upside down, as were her assumptions about her partner.

We can also make assumptions about ourselves. We might think that our vision and goals, both for ourselves and for our relationships, continue to be relevant, when it may be time to rethink and update them so that we can forge ahead with fresh energy and motivation. We might assume that we have done all that is possible to bring about desired results, when there could be other options. We might assume certain limitations about our partner, ourselves or our relationship, when the only thing that is limiting is our assumption.

When Richard and Greta approached the first Christmas together with their new baby they began feeling stressed and angry with each other. Both had assumed that they'd celebrate Christmas the way they'd celebrated it at home. For Richard this involved opening stockings on the morning of Christmas Day; Greta, being German, was used to sitting around the Christmas tree on the 24th in the evening. Until they had talked about their unhappiness, and become aware of the assumptions they'd both been making about the festivities, they'd felt stuck. They could now start compromising and decided to celebrate both ways – candles and carol singing on the evening of the 24th and stockings and turkey on the 25th. Both their Christmases were enriched.

Every time you make an assumption about something you could be missing out. Why did you make that assumption? What did that assumption say about you? Bring curiosity back into your life. Remember your childhood, when the world was new and exciting and you questioned everything. Rediscover that curiosity and shake yourself out of your complacency.

'Appearance
overpowers
even the truth.'

Simonides

Get Curious About Each Other

How would you feel if someone really took an interest? For example imagine if they asked, *'What do you love doing at the weekend?'* and you replied, 'I like going to the sea.' And then imagine they didn't just stop there, and continued to ask you questions: *'What is it about the sea that you like?'* 'It's the peace,' you reply. *'What do you like about peace?'* they ask. 'It makes me calm,' you reply. *'What does that calm do for you?'* they ask. 'It makes me come alive.' *'And what does "coming alive" feel like?'* 'It feels wonderful. Like total freedom.' *'Can I share that with you?'* they ask. 'Of course' you reply.

Most of us would stop after the first question. How many of us would bother or even – go on, admit it – be interested enough in finding out what it was the other person liked about the sea? That kind of interest, in who you are, is rare and to be treasured. If you don't ask questions and don't listen, how much are you missing out on in your knowledge of others – and how much are they missing out on about you?

At the beginning, when meeting someone new, we are curious; we want to ask questions. We have a lifetime to catch up on. Yet our questions can be superficial and never really explore the texture underneath. In long-term relationships our curiosity often stops. We can't believe there's another surprise around the corner. And yet no matter how long (or short) your relationship has been going on for, it's never too late to get interested in your partner – really interested.

Peter was a creature of habit and hated change. When he had to move offices, Janet, his partner, went out of her way to help recreate his working space of the past fifteen years in order, she thought, to reduce the shock of the new. Doors had to be removed to bring in his large antique desk and chair. When he arrived and saw his old office recreated down to the last detail he was disappointed. 'I was looking forward to a complete change, perhaps something modern,' he said. Had Janet taken the time to ask him what he wanted he would have been much happier and she could have saved herself a great deal of effort.

Knowing Me, Knowing You

Let's think about how well you know your partner. Write down what you really know about them. Do the quiz on your own and then go through it together, filling in the gaps and correcting the assumptions.

Partner ....

- Childhood – best thing/worst thing
- Childhood pets
- Childhood homes
- Childhood hobbies
- Favourite childhood book/TV programme/music
- Relatives – likes and dislikes
- First love
- Favourite food
- Favourite sport
- Views on politics
- Views on religion
- Current hobbies
- What relaxes them
- Current worries
- Current great friends
- Favourite music
- Favourite film
- Favourite book
- Favourite food
- Favourite newspaper
- Things they like about work
- Things they dislike about work
- Views on colleagues
- What do they want for the future?
- What job would they do if they could do anything?

Knowing Me, Knowing You/2

Partner ....

- Childhood – best thing/worst thing
- Childhood pets
- Childhood homes
- Childhood hobbies
- Favourite childhood book/TV programme/music
- Relatives – likes and dislikes
- First love
- Favourite food
- Favourite sport
- Views on politics
- Views on religion
- Current hobbies
- What relaxes them
- Current worries
- Current great friends
- Favourite music
- Favourite film
- Favourite book
- Favourite food
- Favourite newspaper
- Things they like about work
- Things they dislike about work
- Views on colleagues
- What do they want for the future?
- What job would they do if they could do anything?

Even More Curious

How curious were you? Did you really know your partner or did you have to make assumptions? Are you good at listening to each other? Do you like being asked about yourself?

If you're in the mood, get even more curious. Take the quiz on to another level.

For example, if your partner answered the question 'What is your favourite food?' with 'Chocolate', ask them what they like about chocolate. If they reply, 'I like the taste and the energy it gives me,' you can ask, 'What do you need the energy for?' If they reply, 'To give me a boost after work,' you could ask why they need a boost after work. It might help you to understand that they find their job very draining and perhaps that's why they often don't want to go out in the evening, or why they are uncommunicative when they get home from work.

You never know where a line of questioning will lead you – and you never will know unless you start. To listen to someone is to give them a gift, but it is only a gift if it's what they want. Always make sure that it's a good time for your partner to enter into a conversation – or in fact to do any exercise in this book. We all need time on our own; be sensitive as to whether or not your partner wants to have a conversation right now. Sometimes just thinking carefully about why your partner is giving a particular answer can lead to greater understanding between you.

If this *is* the right time to communicate, carry on reading. You're about to find out how to listen like an expert and this skill will come in very useful, not only for the rest of this chapter – where you're going to get plenty of chances to listen to each other – but for the rest of your life.

start listening

'The first duty of love is to listen.'

Henry David Thoreau

Active Listening

The basis of any relationship is communication, and being able to listen actively to your partner is an essential skill. You both need to be able to share your thoughts. Surveys have said that most couples only talk together for twelve minutes a day – so prove them wrong.

We can feel unheard in our most intimate relationships. We may find our feelings becoming unmanageable, especially in emotional crises, and if we're not being listened to it can feel very isolating. If you're trying to tell your partner about your hurt feelings, and they are concentrating on the facts of the situation, and not acknowledging your feelings, you may well become even more upset. Not listening properly can be incredibly hurtful.

What is active listening?

Active listening is an intense way of communicating. You can do it with anyone, but it's especially important to do it with your partner. In active listening you focus totally on what the speaker is saying; if your mind is wandering you cannot hear their point of view or take in any information. Listen to what they have to say with an open mind and let them finish before you begin to talk. If you interrupt them, they can feel as though you aren't listening, even if you really are. If you can repeat what they have said, both they and you know you have really heard it. If you are not sure you understand what they have said, then ask them.

You'll notice that once your partner (or whoever you are actively listening to) feels that their messages and feelings have been heard, they will start to relax and therefore have more attention available for listening to you. You can then express your own needs or position. Active listening doesn't mean you have to agree with everything they say. You do not have to avoid revealing how you think and feel about something. You are just showing that you understand and acknowledge what they are saying. It's a very respectful way of communicating.

Rules of active listening

- Maintain eye contact and work at listening – be alert and alive
- Listen optimistically – don't lose interest
- Actively focus your attention on what's being said
- Keep your emotions under control – don't interrupt or jump to conclusions
- Understand and accept what's being said for what it is, independent of your feelings about it
- When they have finished talking, summarise what they said, saying it back to them in your own words. This is to make sure you understood it, and to let them know you were listening
- Look for the feelings or intent beyond the words that were spoken

Benefits of active listening

- It defuses the situation if the other person is angry or hurt, or expressing difficult feelings towards you
- If people are heard and acknowledged, they are often more willing to consider an alternative or back down a little
- People often spot the flaws in their reasoning when they hear their argument played back without criticism
- It helps to identify areas of agreement so that the areas of disagreement are put in perspective and diminished, rather than magnified

'The only true wisdom is in knowing you know nothing.'

Socrates

Family Patterns

Jackie's parents were upset when Jackie announced she was marrying James – a divorced man who was 23 years older than her, and had two children in tow. And yet, in Jackie's opinion, they had no right to be upset because their difference in age was also one of nearly twenty years – something Jackie had never really been aware of because her father always appeared so young and dynamic. When Jackie insisted she was marrying James, no matter what, her parents told her that her father had also been married once before and had already had a child with his first wife, who Jackie had never heard of before.

Even if you know nothing about your family, there are patterns of family relationships that get passed down from generation to generation. As you can see with Jackie, sometimes we're not even aware that we're living our family patterns. These patterns can be as simple as a matter of how we treat friends, how we brush our teeth and the way we react to strangers, or as complex as the ways in which we form and develop our relationships.

Together with these family patterns come family myths. These are stories which originated in our families – the 'family line', as it were, what our strengths and weaknesses are, what routines suit us best and how we feel about illnesses. The important thing to remember is that they are just stories. The more we are told about what our hopes and fears are, how jealous or hard-working we are likely to be, what our belief systems are and how we relate to each other, the more we take these narratives to be true. Our families expect us to be a certain way, and reinforce these expectations with family myths. We may be aware of some of them ('my mother still tells everyone that beetroot makes me ill – but it hasn't for years'). It is those we are not aware of that are more difficult to deal with. In Jackie's case, she was repeating her parents' patterns, but unknowingly.

Becoming aware of these generational patterns allows you to get away from becoming typecast and stuck in a role that you may not feel comfortable in. You can rewrite patterns of the past and allow yourself new endings.

Our Family Tree

By drawing a simple family tree you can find out about your learnt relationship behaviour and your learnt behaviour in general. It will help you to explore relationship stories, and show you which patterns in your family's past are influencing you. It will show you who is important to you and who has been important to you.

Put in as much information about each family member as you want, and think of all the important relationships there are between each of them. It may be enough to look at two generations of your family, or you might want to look at three or four – it's up to you.

You will need to make a family tree for each of you to find out the patterns you both may be stuck in. These trees will bring up unexpected stories, they will help you make connections between seemingly unconnected events and people, and they will show you the behavioural and relationship patterns that have evolved over generations in both of your families.

Be very aware of what you are both thinking and saying as you work through these family trees. Question everything about everyone you include (see page 119). Think about things as seemingly trivial as what similarities there are between you and your grandfather, how your parents might have felt about you if, for example, they had a couple of miscarriages before you were born or if you were born a few days after your grandmother died. Remember what you can about everyone – the fact that someone's brother died a year before he married, or that his father died a year before he divorced may all be relevant. Discover what you can that may have influenced your relationships to date.

Remember that what you don't know might be as important as what you do. Why were you an only child? Why don't you know when your grandfather died or who he was? Don't forget the importance of who comes after you as well as before you – your children, nieces and nephews, grandchildren, stepbrothers and sisters, half-brothers and sisters etc. Think also about the character of each person you write down. What do you know about their temperament, their occupation, their major experiences, their hobbies, their passions? Write it all down. Form as full a picture as you can of everyone in your family tree.

who am I?

A family tree doesn't have to take longer than an hour or so if you don't want it to; you might do it together after a meal or instead of a night of television. It's very bonding to find out about each other's families in this way. The process of drawing the family tree and discussing it is the vital thing – you aren't looking for a 'result', though one may appear. It's a way of questioning old beliefs and stories and finding new ways to look at old predicaments. It will also be a great opportunity for you to listen actively to each other – and explore who you both are.

Bob and Suzy were always collecting waifs and strays and bringing them back to live with their family of five. They liked a busy home and enjoyed new input. Their children, too, were encouraged to bring friends home. It was like an open house. Then Lucy, one of the children's friends, began gradually hanging out with Suzy more and more and helping her with her work. It was the first time that there was tension in the house. The children were jealous of their mum giving all her attention to Lucy. They started being rude and mean to her, and created a really bad atmosphere. Suzy was devastated. She enjoyed the closeness she had with Lucy and didn't know what to do. When she went through her family tree, she made an interesting connection. On remarrying, Suzy's father had adopted his stepdaughter and Suzy now remembered how she and her sister had resented the stepdaughter being with her father all the time. She too had felt jealous. Suzy suddenly felt more understanding towards her children and began setting boundaries around the times she worked with Lucy (see page 112).

Instructions for drawing your family tree

1. Start by drawing yourself as a circle (if female) or square (if male)
2. Add in your partner linked with a single line (relationship) or two parallel lines (marriage)
3. Next, put in your children and any miscarriages or terminations you may have had
4. Then add previous marriages or other important relationships and children from other partners
5. Add your brothers and sisters and their partners and children
6. Above you, add your parents and their other relationships and any stepbrothers or sisters you might have
7. Above them add your grandparents on both sides (and step-grandparents if relevant)
8. Remember to include dates of any marriages, separations, deaths, births, adoptions and miscarriages
9. If there are 'blank bits', think about who you need to talk to in order to be able to fill in the spaces
10. Ask each other the questions on page 119

Charlie always felt that she was rather plain and frumpy. When she looked through her family tree, thinking about each of her relatives in turn, and what they'd thought about her, these feelings were reinforced. Her mother had always handed down her brother's clothes, when Charlie had longed for something beautiful to wear. Her grandparents (on both sides) also hadn't been interested in seeing her as feminine, and never gave her jewellery or anything pretty. It was as if, she felt, she was an ugly duckling and not worth spending any money on. When she got to her aunt, however, Charlie's eyes lit up as she remembered the birthday presents she had been given. 'Oh, my aunt brought me the most beautiful clothes – lots of pinks and bows and all sorts of wonderfully girlie things – and she never called me Charlie. She called me by my proper name, Charlotte.' (See page 114).

My Family Tree

Partner ....

Key

Male ■
Female ●
Relationship —
Marriage =
Miscarriage ▲
Divorce ≠

Suzy's family tree

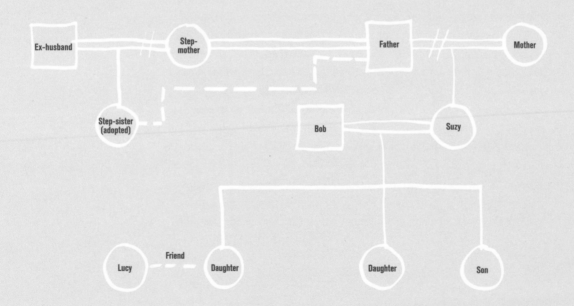

My Family Tree

Partner ....

Key
Male ■
Female ●
Relationship —
Marriage =
Miscarriage ▲
Divorce ≠

Charlie's family tree

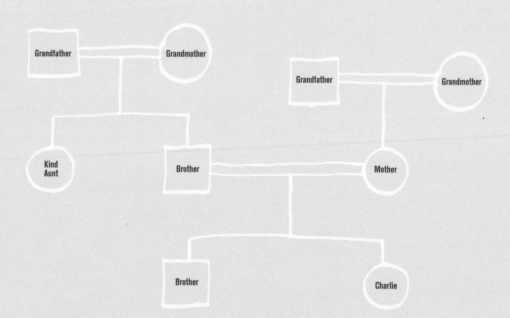

'I am a part of all that I have met.'

Alfred, Lord Tennyson

Family stories

Look at the family tree you have drawn and think about how you live your life through stories. Every time we experience something new we link it up with other personal stories. We then give it a meaning – or several. We have stories about what we're good and bad at, stories about our achievements and failures, stories about our ambitions and laziness and stories about our interests and dislikes. And we have stories about conflict. Whether we believe in these stories depends on how we have linked them together, and what meaning we have given them.

We can even tell different stories about the same event. If Charlie hadn't worked through her entire family tree, she might have created a false memory of a childhood where everyone thought she was plain, and yet this quite categorically wasn't true. By going through her family tree she could access a different perspective. The more different perspectives you can view yourself and your life from, the more you liberate yourself and your relationships.

keep questioning

'To be loved for what one is is rare. The great majority love in others only what they recognise in him of themselves.'

Goethe

Family tree questions

Once you have drawn your family trees, ask each other these kinds of questions. If you have an issue you want to work through, try and keep your questions focused on that theme as much as possible, otherwise your discussion will get too big and you could feel overwhelmed by stories.

About each person on your family tree ask:

- What is/was your relationship to this person?
- What do they/did they think of you and the way you behave to them and others?
- What do they/did they think about the other people on this family tree?
- How did they treat you?

General questions to ask:

- Who else in the family is/was like you?
- Who do you/could you talk to?
- Who taught you to be … (eg under-confident, angry, bullying, loving, secretive etc)?
- Separate yourself out from your parents' beliefs. What are your own?
- Which people on your family tree remind you of your partner?

Relationship roles

At the start of their relationship, Steve had always done the clothes washing as he had a washing machine, and it seemed simpler and friendlier for Joanne to bring her washing to his place than to sit in the laundrette. You might say that Steve took on the role of 'clothes washer'. Once they began living together, Joanne felt it was her duty as the woman to take over the role. Her mother had been the clothes washer in their family and she thought she ought to do it too. But Joanne wasn't her mother and she soon resented washing the clothes. Then one day Steve and Joanne sat together and addressed the issue: why on earth did Joanne have to do the laundry? She had taken on the role – assuming she should as the woman or 'mother'. But it turned out Steve had been quite happy doing it and so he took the role back again.

Almost from the moment we start 'going out' together we slip automatically into roles. It may be that we make assumptions as to which roles we are each going to take up; or it may be that we just automatically slot into roles of our own making; or perhaps we are simply repeating family roles, bringing them into the next generation. In the case of Joanne and Steve, it was only when they consciously decided, together, who was going to do what and why that they both felt satisfied.

Making role assumptions

What roles do you and your partner assume? It could be master/servant, it could be cook/washer-up, it could be bread-winner/parent or even victim/abuser. It could be countless others. We have many different types of roles and, when they work, they make the relationship run smoothly; everything gets done and there's no argument or indecision about who does what. But a role can become a problem if it's too rigid or if you feel you have become it and are trapped by it. Each role does not represent you as a whole – it's just a part of your relationship system. Anyone could take over the role – it's just that you happen to have been doing it and maybe, for some reason, you don't want to any more. Just because, for example, you are the organised, efficient, tidy member of the partnership, it doesn't mean that you should take on the role of the cleaner. It's so easy to say, for example, 'You're hopeless with money, I'll do all our cash management', but what does that do for your partner? Having the role taken away from them means they'll give up all responsibility for money and possibly become even worse at looking after their money than they were before. You may then become stuck with the role of banker and eventually resent them for not being able to share it with you. But they can't, because they are now really bad at looking after money.

When one person is stuck with a role there is no room for spontaneity and a lot of room for bitterness. Keep roles fluid at all times. Keep questioning whether that role is really yours or could be shared. Keep curious about whether you want that role and whether you need it.

Jenny felt one of her roles in the family was that of chauffeur. Her partner, Ed, used to ask her why she had to drive the children everywhere all the time, but he missed the point. If Ed had been realistic he'd have realised that someone had to do it – though perhaps not as often as Jenny did. As soon as Ed appreciated that there was a chauffeur role, and that Jenny felt she had become that role, he began to understand what she was doing and offered to split the driving role with her.

Keep brainstorming about how to handle roles differently. Make sure that you are both clear on what has to be done and how you are going to share roles (or not).

5 major role problems and their solutions
Problem 1: You get fed up with your role: 'I'm sick and tired of ...'
Solution 1: Become more flexible – see if you can't share the role

Problem 2: There's a confusion as to who is filling that role: 'That's my job, you're meant to empty the bin. I change the light bulbs'
Solution 2: Work out who does what and if it really matters as long as certain tasks get accomplished

Problem 3: New roles have to be created: 'Who looks after the baby?'
Solution 3: Work out what these new roles are and then work out how to fill them. Stay flexible – if it's not working, revisit and change it

Problem 4: You're not good at your role: 'I never pay the bills on time'
Solution 4: Share the role between the two of you, let your partner show you how to accomplish the role or hand the role over to them. You could also give the role to a third party or just check if the role is still necessary

Problem 5: The role is taken away: 'I'm better at it than you ...'
Solution 5: If you agree then that's fine. If you disagree, see if you could share it

'When I let go of
what I am, I become
what I might be.'

Lao Tzu

Taking The Role Off

If you feel boxed into a role, for example that of bread-winner or organiser, why not play a game around it?

In order to discuss a role, start by separating it out from both of you. Imagine taking it off – like an item of clothing – and putting it on a chair in front of both of you. Why not write down the role, for example, 'food organiser' and put it on the chair. Both you and your partner should now think about the role and mention at least one thing that's useful to each of you about it.

The person whose role it is can then talk about what it feels like no longer having that role. They may feel anxious about leaving it in case it isn't filled, but it's important to trust that it will be. Talk to your partner about what you'd like to happen and ask them what they'd like to happen. Maybe the role can be divided into several smaller ones, perhaps it could be taken up by your partner or maybe there's no longer any need for it. Or maybe this is an ideal time to start compromising (see page 160). Sometimes roles are so tied in together that questioning one role will throw up lots of other questions about others.

Be honest and open. Keep calm and constructive. If you can't solve the role in one sitting, why not agree to share it until something can be worked out? What would it feel like to take it in turns?

Curious Us is all about ... assumptions that we make about ourselves
and others
getting curious about each other
checking out how well we really know each other
listening to each other properly
finding out about our family patterns and myths
working out how best to divide up the roles
within our relationship

waking up

5

conscious us

Mirror Images

Let's start thinking about you, and who you are, by exploring who your partner is. The next exercise is about exploring aspects of you that you have in common with your partner; because the characteristics we like and dislike, and sometimes criticise, in others are often characteristics we share with them. The character traits in others that you think you can't see in yourself may well be in there somewhere.

For example, if you admire your partner's energy, but don't feel very energetic yourself, keep a diary for a week of all you accomplish in a day and the energy you need to do all that. It may be that the energy doesn't seem similar at first. Maybe your partner goes out jogging and kick-boxing and swimming, and you feel that all you do is stay at home and sit at your desk and work. You don't feel energetic at all compared to your partner. But just think of the energy you are using in your brain. Become aware that your energies are different, but that you do share that characteristic.

Similarly your partner's untidiness may drive you mad, but are you sure it isn't a trait that you share with them? Indeed you might even have been attracted to them because you shared that characteristic. Their messiness might have made you feel better about yourself ('At least I'm not as messy as them'), but it's now got out of hand and you feel irritated by it. Take responsibility for sharing in the characteristic. Admit that it's a problem you have too and see what you can do about it together.

'One of the things that really annoys me about you, David,' said Keith, 'is that you never say "No" to anybody. You constantly want to give. You get insane pleasure out of baking a cake for someone at 6am because you've agreed to see them that morning – when I wanted you to be doing something for us.' 'But Keith,' said David, 'you can't say "No" either. Just look at your diary. When I want to have some time together – just the two of us – you don't have a minute that isn't taken up already. You say "Yes" to anyone who asks you to do anything and get excited by having a full diary. Saying "No" is your issue as well.'

Once they realised that they shared the same characteristic, although they showed it in different ways, Keith and David could work towards accommodating it. Keith decided that he'd leave at least one evening a week free for the two of them to be at home together and one evening free for them to go out. He'd become aware of why he was saying 'Yes', to everything and learn to say 'No' to things that he really didn't want to do. David also agreed to saying 'No'. He would put himself and Keith first – above his relationship with other people who were making demands on him. Furthermore, David realised that by making himself so busy he was avoiding confronting what might be wrong with the relationship.

Partner ....

First tell my partner all the characteristics they have that I appreciate (write them down too)

These characteristics are also true of me.
Do I recognise those characteristics?

How do they reveal themselves in me?

How could I use these characteristics in my life right now?

Partner ....

**First tell my partner all the characteristics they have that I appreciate
(write them down too)**

....

**These characteristics are also true of me.
Do I recognise those characteristics?**

....

How do they reveal themselves in me?

....

How could I use these characteristics in my life right now?

....

'Everything that irritates us about others can lead us to an understanding of ourselves.' **Carl Jung**

Sharing Characteristics

Remember that this exercise is all about exploring yourself and your characteristics, not about blaming (or dumping on) your partner.

Partner ....

First tell your partner all the characteristics they have that you find difficult (write them down too)

(eg angry)

These characteristics are also true of me. Do I recognise them?

(eg Do I think I'm angry? Yes, I lose my temper sometimes)

How do they reveal themselves in me?

(eg I can get very angry if things don't go my way)

How could I use these characteristics in my life right now?

(eg I could use the energy of my anger to tidy up the kitchen)

Partner ....

First tell your partner all the characteristics they have that you find difficult (write them down too)

(eg stubborn)

These characteristics are also true of me. Do I recognise them?

(eg Do I think I'm stubborn? No, not really)

How do they reveal themselves in me?

(eg I suppose I can be very determined to eat healthily)

How could I use these characteristics in my life right now?

(eg I could be stubborn and persistent in making my business succeed)

It Takes Two

You've probably found that you share more characteristics than you realised. This is the first step towards understanding how pointless blaming someone else is. Often our own issues become the things that annoy us most about others.

Through blame, we can easily become a victim and hand power over to our partner: 'If only they'd pay me more attention, I'd be much happier …' or, 'If only they'd do what I say, I wouldn't need to shout.' But you're not a victim. This is your relationship as well, and once you are able to see the part you play in *your* relationship – once you become conscious of your relationship – you can set boundaries for what you want and what you don't want.

Norah worked hard. She had her own business and really enjoyed working long hours. She basically wanted to work all the time. But Pete was affected by this and resented it. Pete became the victim in the relationship; 'If only she'd stop working so hard,' he'd say. 'We don't see enough of each other.' He blamed Norah for everything that was going wrong between them.

Rather than blame Norah for working hard, Pete had to take responsibility for how he was feeling, and accept that it was *his* issue and not hers. Pete had to acknowledge that he was upset that they weren't spending enough time together. He had to decide what he wanted and what he could tolerate. He had to realise he was in control of the situation.

These are some of the questions that Pete asked himself:
- Is Norah working so hard a permanent problem or a blip?
- What can I do while Norah is out working?
- Can I help her with her work?
- Do I feel rejected?
- Could Norah change the hours that she works?
- Could I change the hours that I work?
- Do I feel envy?
- What do I want from Norah?

Luckily Pete didn't destroy the love that he had with Norah. He avoided blame, respected her position, compromised and stayed friends with her – keys to having a good relationship. He didn't criticise, instead he expressed his feelings honestly and told her how the problem felt to him. Pete realised that he wanted attention and decided that he would look for it from others as well as Norah. Once he backed off, she began to miss his attention and slowly changed her working patterns so that they could see more of each other.

Remember, you should be looking to work on your *own* feelings and expectations rather than trying to change your partner. Whatever your partner does that you don't like, you have to work through on your own and decide if you can live with it by changing yourself. If, for example, your partner never listens to you, maybe you can find a way of communicating more effectively. Similarly, if your partner is very critical, you could find a way of taking their criticism less personally. You can only take responsibility in a relationship for the part you play.

Once your partner knows that you are feeling unhappy about something, they may be able to work with you to think of a compromise – that key word is at the heart of conscious relationships. And, if you change your behaviour, then often you will find that the behaviour of your partner will shift in some way too.

'As soon as you have made a thought, laugh at it.' **Lao Tzu**

Enjoying Your Differences

Make a list overleaf of all your partner's shortcomings; be as honest as possible. This is meant to be a fun exercise, so go for it in a light-hearted way – it's good for you to let rip. Look at the list and at each of the things that annoy you. Might they possibly be things you recognise in yourself? Ask yourself how you could change so that their behaviour doesn't upset you; what could you do that will stop you being annoyed by them? What could be endearing about that 'short-coming'? Could it remind you of a cartoon character, a character from a book, a film character or even someone else you know? If you can laugh at your irritations with each other so much the better. Bear in mind that some of us find it more difficult to laugh at ourselves than others.

Ed was always forgetting everything at home. He had an extremely high-powered career, but once he got home he resorted to being a child. Invariably he lost his wallet every morning. By nicknaming him 'Mr Wallet Man', Pam managed to keep her temper and see this foible as a part of Ed rather than the annoyance it was to her. Needless to say it was Pam's fairly regular losing of her bag that probably made her so annoyed about Ed's forgetfulness.

Rather than making demands on your partner or expecting anything from them, look at your partner's shortcomings as an aspect of their character and personality. The things that annoy you about your partner are part of their charm – possibly the reason you fell for them in the first place. Your partner needs to feel liked and accepted as they are. We're all different, do things differently, have different motivations and needs – celebrate that.

Partner ....

Write down one or two of your partner's shortcomings

....

....

Then, think of an affectionate nickname for them

....

....

Partner ....

Write down one or two of your partner's shortcomings

....

....

Then, think of an affectionate nickname for them

....

....

Work On Your Relationship

Be honest. If you're unhappy, tell your partner what you'd like – they can't read your mind. Don't suffer in silence. Talk to each other. Invest time in your relationship. At work you may do team-building exercises or go on bonding weekends to improve communication and the quality of your professional relationships. Do the same sort of thing with your partner. Spend time together, appreciate each other, care for each other, surprise each other, listen to each other, let each other know what works – and what doesn't. Share new experiences. Be two individuals who enjoy sharing time together, rather than two people leaning on each other and propping each other up. Build awareness, not necessarily agreement.

A conscious relationship is ...
- When you love yourself enough to believe that any potential partner is lucky to have met you
- When you're not looking for someone to make you feel complete
- When you are true to yourself and don't feel that you have to be something that you're not
- When you can see your partner for who they really are – not who you would like them to be
- When you know what you want
- When you understand that you are in control of your relationship – it's no-one else's fault if things go wrong

Remember that even problematic relationships give you the chance to become stronger as you overcome the problems they throw at you.

Conscious Relationships

In the same way that you 'took your role off' to be able to see it clearly (page 124), try now to think about 'the relationship' as a separate entity that you can 'take off' and work on objectively.

Thinking of the relationship as separate is a great way of beginning to shift the blame away from both of you. The relationship can be represented by an object placed on the table in front of you to help make it more tangible. It'll help you look in a more detached way at how you are together and at any issues you may have, and encourage the two of you to think about your relationship as something you both have a stake in.

Why not start by asking the relationship these ten questions, adding to them as and when you feel like it. Work on this together if you like.

1. What does this relationship look like?

2. What hopes do we both have for the relationship?

3. What fears do we both have for the relationship?

4. How do we both get on with this relationship?

5. What have we never said or done in this relationship – what is taboo?

6. What would happen to this relationship if we changed that?

7. What could we do to improve this relationship?

8. When could we make time to improve this relationship?

9. How do other people see our relationship?

10. Do we have any relationship left?

Making Time

When you're in a relationship you need time, for the two of you to be alone together.

But making time in a busy life can be difficult. Check your diary and see what you can get out of. Can you delegate? Do you have to attend that breakfast meeting or dinner? Do you really want to see that friend? Are you keeping these commitments at the expense of the two of you? Are you organising a busy schedule to avoid making time for your relationship – or yourself?

Jim and Anna were having sexual problems. Jim was a workaholic and spent almost every night of the week out – either with colleagues or at work – only arriving home when Anna was asleep. However, at the weekend he wanted to make love with Anna. His week was over and he was ready for the weekend. By the end of the week, on the other hand, Anna saw Jim as a stranger. To her it seemed that for five days of the week they'd hardly seen each other and she felt she needed time to get to know him again before having sex. The result was that Anna didn't want to make love. This was building up into a problem.

It seems calculating to schedule in time to be with those you love, and yet it's essential if it doesn't already happen of its own accord. A romantic walk through the park once a week or a drink in the pub and a good, long chat isn't all that's necessary, but it is necessary. Otherwise even the closest of relationships can drift apart.

Keep your relationship buoyant by:
- **Prioritising your diary and ditching unnecessary commitments**
- **Making time for yourself, and for you and your partner**
- **Understanding how much intimacy and how much freedom you each want – it changes all the time**
- **Having difficult conversations (eg about sex) so that you can understand how the other feels**

Conscious Faces

This exercise requires you to snuggle up close and avoid getting self-conscious. Just have fun. Become aware of each other's faces. When was the last time you really looked at each other? Suspend disbelief and play a little game with each other. Sunday morning in bed might be a good time.

1. Sit up really close to your partner and choose a feature of their face that you like or are curious about
2. Describe to them what you like or find interesting about that particular feature
3. How does it make you feel?
4. Mention that feeling to them
5. Now make up a story about what could happen in your relationship if that feeling was your priority
6. Tell your story to your partner and ask them what they felt as they heard your story
7. Now swap so that your partner does the same thing to you
8. Next imagine both of those feelings working together – what could these feelings bring into your relationship?

If you have time, do the same exercise but this time think about your partner's clothes. Choose outfits of theirs that you particularly like or find interesting. How do these outfits make you feel? Think again about what could happen in your relationship if that feeling was prevalent.

Carol and Alan had been in a relationship for a long time and were feeling a little bored with each other. It had been a long time since they'd really looked at each other or shared their intimate thoughts. Looking at Alan's face, Carol chose the creases round Alan's eyes to focus on. They looked crinkly and like the crevasses in the side of a mountain. They made her want to explore and go on more adventures with him, spend weekends visiting new places, bring more spontaneity into their lives.

get inspired

'What lies behind us, and what lies before us are tiny matters compared to what lies within us.'

Ralph Waldo Emerson

Alan chose Carol's nose to focus on and described it as making him feel 'safe and comforted'. His story was of the two of them sitting in front of the fire eating toast all snuggled up together. Alan and Carol realised that they'd not really been doing that much together recently and that they missed those times – particularly when visiting friends in the countryside. They decided to book in with some of these old friends so they could have comfortable times together in front of warm fires with a few adventures thrown in. They both felt inspired to spend more time together doing things they hadn't done for a while.

What Did We Enjoy?

Often the activities that once bound us together fall by the wayside. It could be that we move, become too busy, have children. Now is a great time to remember what it was you enjoyed, to work out what happened to those activities that bound you together and how to bring them back into your lives.

The happiest relationships can consist of two people who don't appear to have any interests in common, yet if you dig deep you may find they both love catching falling leaves in Autumn or swimming in icy lakes in Summer. You don't have to both love trainspotting or reading historical biographies to have a great relationship.

Make a list of as many things as you can that you used to enjoy doing together. Write the list quickly (eg cooking, going to the cinema, making love, kite flying, talking, reading to each other, running marathons etc). And include friends you used to enjoy seeing.

What we enjoy doing together and who we enjoy seeing	Tick the ones we've stopped doing/seeing	What's stopped us doing/seeing them?

Now work out how you could bring them back into your life.
When are you going to start?

Feel The Fun

There's nothing better than just saying 'Yes' and doing something on the spur of the moment. Spontaneity is a habit and, if you've forgotten how to be spontaneous, you can easily bring it back into your life.

We sometimes have to plan to put the fun back into our lives, because we've got no time for it. But it's essential to have spontaneity. A life without spontaneity is too safe and boring; relationships become stale and stagnant. To be truly alive we want both the safety of routine and the excitement of random, unexpected things happening. Sometimes we've become so 'grown-up' it's difficult to remember what fun is and how to throw ourselves into it rather than holding back.

Think back to what was fun when you were a child and what was fun for both of you in the early stages of your relationship. Reintroducing fun into a relationship that's not fully functioning can be difficult and feel awkward. You may not want to play together any more or make a fool of yourself – or maybe you're frightened your partner will say 'No'. You, yourself, might even feel frightened of doing something you haven't done for ages, like making love in the bathroom.

So, how do you burst through that fear? The only way to do it is to let go of your old feelings. If you act differently, you'll feel different. Remember back to a time when, say, a child asked you to play with them and you didn't feel like it, but once you joined in you really enjoyed doing it. Well, it's the same for all fun. Just dive in. If you do it wholeheartedly you'll enjoy it and very soon it too will become familiar and safe again.

Although John and Robyn had chosen to live by the sea, in the last five years Robyn had begun to stay at home a lot. After her children were born, she began to feel happiest lying on her bed with a good book, and when John took the children off to the beach every weekend for the day, Robyn breathed a sigh of relief and got back into bed with her latest novel. Even though a little bit of her wanted to go out with them, she almost feared that she'd enjoy it so much she'd miss out on her time alone, reading.

Then one day, Robyn decided she would go to the beach. She even took her swimming costume. What's more, John persuaded her to go for a swim.

Robyn hadn't been in the water for years. She loved it. It reminded her of her past and together they stayed in the water for ages. It was as if the spell had been broken.

Sometimes it's difficult to remember what you used to enjoy – what your dreams were. Just keep listening carefully to each other. Throw-away comments like, 'I always loved going go-kart racing when I was a child', or, 'I used to love eating Mum's cake mix', reveal your secret wishes and dreams. Keep a list of each other's wishes and give each other what the other wants, rather than what you *think* they want.

Make a time and a place to have fun – or just go for it. Take your partner by surprise. You'll never look back.

Conscious Us is all about ...   seeing what characteristics we have in common

enjoying our differences

realising that we can only take responsibility
for ourselves

working with the relationship

making time for us

looking at each other remembering what
we enjoyed

becoming spontaneous all over again

working together

6

team us

Our Team

With each chapter, your relationship is growing. You've become curious about how the other thinks, you've become conscious about how you and your partner behave in a relationship and about having control over your feelings. Now you can think about being part of a team and how that works.

This chapter is about teamwork; building a relationship based on honesty, openness, friendship and compromise – a winning combination.

Holidays are key times to reconnect with each other, but during the average day there are several key points when we do (or could) interact with each other. These are times for friendship. Start by thinking, together, about these times and what you'd like to happen in them – because differences in how you want to play them can easily occur.

These are the times when you can really consolidate yourselves as a team:

- **Saying hello in the morning**
- **Saying goodbye when leaving in the morning**
- **Planning and cooking meals**
- **Dividing up household chores and childcare**
- **Meeting up at the end of the day**
- **Planning and then doing something together**
- **Going out spontaneously**

Sometimes a simple tweak to your team is all that's required to make things start working again. You've already done a lot of work on the good things about your relationship; you're going to start this chapter by thinking about what isn't right and what's missing. Sadly this is often easier than thinking about what is right.

Blurt

For this exercise just blurt out all the things you wish your partner would do. Go wild – write down everything from emptying the dustbin to giving you a massage. If you hold yourselves back you won't achieve anything. Remember this is about learning what you both want.

Unless you are really specific, nothing will ever change. 'I wish you would make me feel loved', or, 'I wish you'd pay more attention to me', are too vague to be of any use when working on your relationship. Get as accurate as possible about what you want. Once you've both blurted it all out, show each other your list. Then make sure you keep asking each other questions until you know exactly what you both want.

Remember to keep your feedback to facts and how they impact on you. This is not about blame, this is about solving problems as a team. And, why not soften each blow with a compliment first?

eg
'I love it when we go out together, but I wish you'd be on time.'
'What specifically would you like?'
'I'd like you to be punctual whenever we're doing anything together.'
'What else would you like?'
'If you can't be punctual I'd like you to phone me in good time and let me know.'

eg
'I know you love me as much as I love you, but I wish you'd act as if you loved me.'
'What specifically would you like?'
'We used to kiss each other goodbye in the morning and I'd like us to do that again.'
'What else would you like?'
'I'd like us to fall asleep in each other's arms like we used to.'
'Anything else?'

and so on …

'Love seems the swiftest, but it is the slowest of all growths. No man or woman really knows what perfect love is until they have been married a quarter of a century.'

Mark Twain

Constructive Blurting

The moment you've finished this exercise, go straight on to the next one. Make sure you have time for both. End on a high.

Partner ....

Complete these sentences

I love ……………..………………..…….but I wish you'd ……………………..……………..

What specifically would I like? ……..……………………………..…..……………..

What else would I like? ……………..………………..……………………..…………..

I love ……………..………………..……. but I wish you'd ……………………..…………..

What specifically would I like? ……..……………………………..…..……………..

What else would I like? ……………..………………..……………………..…………..

I love ……………..………………..……. but I wish you'd ……………………..…………..

What specifically would I like? ……..……………………………..…..……………..

What else would I like? ……………..………………..……………………..…………..

Choose one thing you'd like to start changing this week and decide when you're going to do it.

Constructive Blurting/2

The moment you've finished this exercise, go straight on to the next one. Make sure you have time for both. End on a high.

Partner ....

Complete these sentences

I love ………………...…………...…….but I wish you'd ……………………………...…………..

What specifically would I like? ………...……………...………………………..…...……………..

What else would I like? ……………..………………...……………………..…...…………..

I love ………………...……………...…... but I wish you'd ……………………………...…………..

What specifically would I like? ………...……………...………………………..…...……………..

What else would I like? ……………..………………...……………………..…...…………..

I love ………………...……………...…... but I wish you'd ……………………………...…………..

What specifically would I like? ………...……………...………………………..…...……………..

What else would I like? ……………..………………...……………………..…...…………..

Choose one thing you'd like to start changing this week and decide when you're going to do it.

I Love It When ...

After all that honesty, you'll want some reinforcement. Without a pause,
complete these sentences for each other and then spend some time telling
each other all the things you love about each other. This will feel better.

Partner ....

I love it when ....

I love it when ....

I love it when ....

I love it when ....

I love it when ....

I love it when ....

I love it when ....

I love it when ....

I love it when ....

'There is only one happiness in life, to love and be loved.'

George Sand

I Love It When .../2

Partner ....

I love it when ....

I love it when ....

I love it when ....

I love it when ....

I love it when ....

I love it when ....

I love it when ....

I love it when ....

I love it when ....

United We Stand

Within a partnership, as in any team, there are always lots of decisions to make. When you make any decision it's essential to take the feelings and opinions of both of you into account. The best way to reach a solution is usually to compromise – when you keep talking until you reach an agreement, so that you're both sharing the decision-making and the power. Sometimes, of course, one or the other of you really doesn't care what the outcome is, in which case the one who does care can decide. Listening to your intuition will always tell you whether the decision that's been made is the right one for you. If it's not, start discussing it again.

Money is often a subject over which compromises have to be made. Once again, so long as you take the other's feelings and opinions into account, you can make it work.

Vicky and Sam were moving in together. Vicky was high earning and enjoyed spending her money, but Sam was lower earning and more cautious. Sam was worried about the mortgage that Vicky wanted them to share, and about the way Vicky wanted their home to be decorated. Sam felt that he could probably get a better deal than Vicky could as he cared more about looking after their money. Vicky was worried Sam was going to be too penny-pinching and that their home wouldn't look good.

They found a compromise by dividing their financial duties according to who was better at what. Sam was better at negotiating cheap deals, so he was put in charge of getting quotes from suppliers. Vicky compromised her views on just how she wanted their home to look in order to economise, and by negotiating cheaper deals on what Vicky wanted, Sam felt that their money was being well spent.

'Compromise, if not the spice of life, is its solidity. It is what makes nations great and marriages happy.'

Anonymous

Celebrate Compromise

There are always things that are so essential to our values, we really don't feel we can give in on them. It might be something emotionally complex; you could never tell a white lie to anyone and yet that's what your partner wants you to do. Or it might be something to do with where your duties lie, for example that you feel it's essential to invite all your family to your wedding rather than just some of them, and yet your partner doesn't want them all to be there. Whatever it is that you can't compromise on will depend on the problem.

If you and your partner have something that you're not seeing eye to eye about, see if you can solve it here by answering these six questions together and then by filling in the Compromise Circles.

1. What do you and your partner not see eye to eye on?

2. What would compromise be like for each of you?

3. What would stop you from compromising?

4. What would happen if you did compromise?

5. What would it feel like?

Compromise Circles

Both write in the inner circle overleaf what you can't give in on, so that
you'll know exactly where you both stand. Then, in the outer circle,
think about all the things you *can* compromise on. By understanding
the other's bottom line you'll know the boundaries of the situation. The
outside circle is where you put your negotiations. If you still feel stuck,
read on until you understand each other's points of view.

eg **Partner**	**'I always go skiing at Christmas'**
Partner	**'I love Christmas at home and hate skiing'**
Inner circle	(things we can't give in on)
Partner	**'I must have a skiing holiday'**
Partner	**'I must have Christmas at home'**
Outer circle	(things we can compromise about)
Partner	**'It doesn't have to be at Christmas'**
Partner	**'I'm prepared to put up with a skiing holiday at another time'**

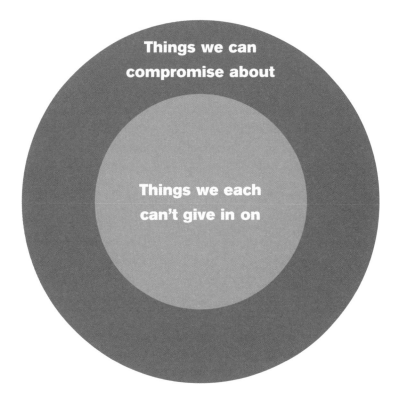

What's Your Point Of View?

Sometimes when we understand each other's differences they no longer seem weird or irritating. But in order to understand our differences we have to take time to listen and learn. Every now and then it is a good idea to treat our partners as if we've never met them before, ask their point of view and how they see the situation. Only then can you both decide what to do. Frequently, just hearing what the other thinks is enough to solve the situation.

Nancy and David had been together for years and Nancy often got annoyed about the state of their kitchen. After enjoying a meal together, which she had cooked, Nancy liked having the kitchen clean and tidy. David, on the other hand, wanted to get on with whatever he was doing and clear the kitchen up later. For Nancy, the kitchen was a place of chaos, a chore that hung over her until she did it. She hated the way David just left the mess until later – and never really trusted that he would clear it up. The result was that she usually did it herself. In her eyes she was cooking and clearing for a thoroughly unhelpful partner.

From David's viewpoint Nancy was making a fuss. He was happy to clear the kitchen, but liked doing it whilst listening to the news. The news was on the radio at 10pm and by leaving the kitchen clear-up until 10pm, David could multi-task – catch up on the news whilst pottering around tidying up the kitchen. It meant he had a legitimate excuse for listening to his radio.

Nancy had never bothered to ask David before why he left the clearing up until later, and was amazed to hear this rational argument. Once she had heard David's point of view, she was more than happy to leave the mess until 10pm, knowing he would then clear it up.

Each of us has our own viewpoint on the world and when we find out what our partner's viewpoint is we can really learn about them and find the solution that we're looking for. Get curious about what your partner sees and feels. Take a moment to see the world from their point of view. It's fascinating.

Their viewpoint isn't right or wrong, it's just different, but in order to understand it you have to become totally open about the way you think and completely prepared to listen. By sharing your viewpoints you can move forward, because in each of your positions there will be things that the other can appreciate and embrace. When you explore, you're not necessarily trying to solve anything, you're just discovering as much as you can so that you'll have a better understanding and appreciation of each other.

the best of both worlds

'Every man takes
the limits of his own
field of vision for the
limits of the world.'

Arthur Schopenhauer

Exploring viewpoints

Pick a calm time to do this exercise, and choose a problem that's upsetting you at the moment to work through. Take it in turns to describe your point of view about the problem. Then think about which parts of each other's points of view you can understand and agree with. These new, shared points of view can be brought into the joint viewpoint that you are creating together.

Before you start, make an agreement between the two of you – discuss:

1. What problem do we want to think about?
2. Are we able to let go of our positions and be open?
3. Are we both happy to respect the other's viewpoint?
4. Can we agree that there's no 'right' or 'wrong', just two differing points of view?

Now, look at the issue, and take it in turns to ask each other these questions:

1. What from your point of view is important?
2. What do I need to know to understand your viewpoint better?
3. What's important to you about holding that viewpoint and why do you hold it?
4. What do you want to happen?

Next, think about each other's points of views and ask yourselves:

1. What do I like about my partner's viewpoint?
2. What does my partner's viewpoint offer?

Now each write down what you've learnt from the other. If you're not seeing things from the other's point of view at all, then stop for a while and come back to this exercise at a later date.

Our viewpoint

Think about 'our viewpoint'. You want to create a team, a partnership that combines the best of both of you. Ask each other these four questions:

1. What have you told me about your viewpoint that I would like to bring into our shared viewpoint?
2. In our shared viewpoint, how would things be different from our separate viewpoints?
3. What could we add to our viewpoint that neither of us have in our original viewpoints?
4. What could we do in the future using our new viewpoint?

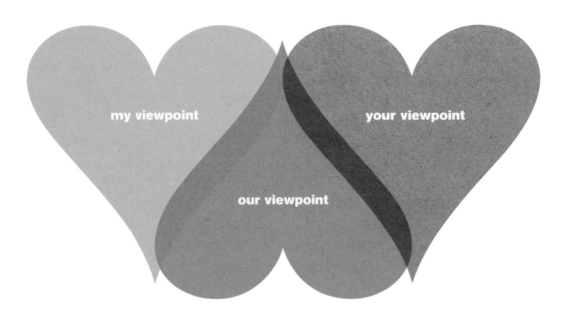

my viewpoint

your viewpoint

our viewpoint

What Makes A Great Relationship?

There are many things that make a great relationship. Understanding each other is key; being aware of each other, growing together, learning how to compromise and seeing each other's viewpoints are also important. It could be your friendship that makes you a great couple – the mutual respect and enjoyment of each other that you share; it could be your confidence together or the way you intuitively feel about each other.

Sometimes thinking about other couples can give you an understanding of where you want to be. This exercise is to do together.

Make a list of at least three couples that you respect and admire (they can be real or not). You don't both have to respect and admire them, as long as one of you does. And you don't have to respect and admire everything about them, just think of something they have that in your eyes makes their relationship special.

Next to each couple write down what you think it is that makes them such a good team. For example, you might think that the love Romeo and Juliet had was special because they were so impetuous, spontaneous and reckless. Then think about what you could do to bring some of those qualities into your relationship.

Couple	What we think makes their relationship work
....	....
....	....
....	....
....	....
....	....

What could we do to bring some of those qualities into out relationship?

Think about who you are now as a team and what you want from your life together. Using either this page or a larger sheet of paper, do a collage together of your life in the future.

This is a great opportunity to really think about your hopes and dreams. Let your mind go, find pictures and words that trigger your imagination. Just enjoy yourselves and let your thoughts flow.

Why not ...
- Look in magazines and cut out your dream home or holiday
- Stick in menus from your favourite restaurants
- Add pictures of your friends and family, or people you would like to meet
- Add words, slogans or the lyrics of a special song or poem
- Add glitter or feathers for glamour

You don't have to fill both pages if you don't want to. Do what you feel is right.

If only ...

Every so often William would cut extravagantly beautiful photographs of expensive diamond necklaces, or exquisite handbags, out of a magazine and leave them on the table for Alice to find with little notes saying things like, 'This is what you really deserve', or, 'If only you could wear this for me'. You can imagine how indulged Alice felt. The fact that they had no money didn't stop their fantasies.

Team Us is all about ...   consolidating the team
constructively working on what you want
giving feedback on exactly what you like
understanding compromise
looking at and combining each other's
    viewpoints
creating a great team
making a collage of our team
fantasising together

stormy times ahead

7

rocky us

'Smooth seas
do not make
skilful sailors.'

Anonymous

Conflict Is Natural

We can be in different phases of a relationship to each other at a given time. This chapter is all about equipping you with the tools to help you weather the storms that inevitably blow up in any relationship. The exercises that follow should provide invaluable self-awareness about how to cope with conflict. Many things can play their part in altering how you feel about each other and they can come from both inside and outside the relationship. It's normal to go through stormy weather, but most of us have only got our parents' relationship and our own previous relationships as examples to guide us.

Nicholas was the child of a stable, happy home and had no fears about going into a marriage. Sarah's parents, on the other hand, had separated almost the moment she was born. So Sarah had grown up in a single-parent family and had never consciously seen a successful partnership at work. Her marital role models were American TV shows of the sixties in which everyone had a happy marriage. There were no such things as rows, only humour and perfection. When Nicholas and Sarah had their first row, Sarah was certain it was the end of their marriage. Even though Nicholas tried to convince her that rows were normal and would ultimately help them strengthen their relationship, she couldn't believe him. It took a while, and Nicholas had to keep pressing the point home, but eventually Sarah came to appreciate the depth of their love for each other, and she understood, thanks to Nicholas's teaching, that the occasional spat meant nothing and actually strengthened their bond.

For those of us without living, breathing role models, celluloid memories can heavily influence the way we think about relationships. We imagine that the romantic period of our relationship will go on for ever. But sooner or later things start going 'wrong'. Conflict is natural. It's when a relationship becomes conscious. It's us trying to get our needs met – wanting to win the fight and feeling angry, irritated and resentful. Disagreeing is an essential part of bonding a relationship. Through dealing with arguments and rows – even silent ones – we become more whole.

Throwing Stones

As your relationship matures you will begin to understand what can trigger a row and how to deal with it. If your relationship is strong, you will also know that although you may disagree about this particular issue, fundamentally you share enough to be able to withstand any damage from the row and heal any rift.

There are crisis times in any relationship and particular things that are more likely than not to cause conflict. Below are two lists, one of crisis times (see if you've got any coming up) and one of behaviour that can cause conflict. Forewarned is forearmed.

Possible crisis times in a relationship:
- **New baby** – exhausting and distracting
- **Career** – career v. home, career v. children
- **Change** – both organic and deliberate (midlife crisis, moving house)
- **Children** – from education to empty nest
- **Dreams** – the vision you built up for the future isn't happening
- **Friendships** – with others, do they impinge too much?
- **Home** – money, time, clutter
- **Housework** – division of labour, do you take it in turns?
- **Money** – spending v. security, power
- **Relatives** – in-laws, elderly parents
- **Traditions, celebrations** – birthdays, anniversaries

Behaviour that can cause conflict:
- **Acting like a victim** – casting your partner as unreasonable and dominating
- **Blame** – blaming your partner when things go wrong
- **Bullying** – aggressive behaviour towards partner
- **Contempt** – when you have no respect for your partner
- **Criticism** – attacking who your partner is, their character and personality
- **Cynicism** – low-grade detachment
- **Defensiveness** – when the problem isn't me, it's you

- **Jealousy** – past/future loves
- **Power** – emotional, sexual or material
- **Sarcasm** – the lowest form of scorn
- **Stone-walling** – avoiding both a fight and the marriage
- **Stress** – bringing work stress home
- **Tiredness** – emotional and physical exhaustion

Grrrrrr ...

For most people rows are inevitable and, in a worst-case scenario, can end up with the two of you not talking to each other, living parallel lives and feeling very lonely. When we're in the middle of these rows it can feel bleak – we don't allow new information to come in, our minds go round in circles. We think in exaggerated and black and white terms, 'I never ...', 'You always ...'.

Once you understand what triggers your rows you can begin to see how your reaction to the original row can provoke further rows. By taking a step back, you become an onlooker and can view your own relationship from a more detached point of view. You may also be able to decide to take the first steps towards changing.

These next two exercises will help you understand each other better. Work on them together, avoiding blame. They're about solving problems as a partnership. As the American philosopher William James said, 'Whenever you're in conflict with someone, there is one factor that can make the difference between damaging your relationship and deepening it. That factor is attitude.' If you can, laugh together – either to end a row or whilst answering these questions, or any time you can. Laughter is a great healer.

When you have finished each exercise, take time to thank each other. It's good that you can allow yourselves to be so honest with each other.

making up

Purrr ...

Ask each other these questions:

What usually triggers a row?

What annoys us about each other, what behaviour would we like instead?

What have you got to do or say to get me going – or not do or say?

What do I have to do or say to get you angry – or not do or say?

What do I bottle up and haven't told you about?

What do you bottle up and haven't told me about?

What could I do to make you happier, to defuse the row?

What could you do to make me happier, to defuse the row?

How could we behave differently?

How would anyone know that we were behaving differently?

When shall we start behaving differently?

Don't Let The Sun Go Down On Your Wrath

In a relationship, there is no 'right' or 'wrong'. It's not about the truth, or blame. It's about understanding each other. Listening to your partner when they are upset with you doesn't mean you are 'giving in', rather it takes strength and courage. Ending an evening sleeping alone on the sofa is not the way forward in a relationship.

When you're calm, and not in the heat of an argument, get together with a large bowl or basket in front of both of you and a huge pile of scrap paper. Imagine the bowl is your relationship and have a conversation with it, questioning its very existence or solving the problem you are having right now. Every time you want to ask it something scrunch up a piece of the scrap paper. Then throw the paper into the bowl and try to answer the question. The paper chucking will help you relax and make light of the issue. Become a team working together on resolving the issue and, like a team would, hug each other at the end of the game. Here are some sample questions to start you off, then make up some of your own.

Scrunch paper up and ask the question
What's more important – arguing over this problem or our relationship?
Throw the paper into the bowl and take it in turns to answer the question

Scrunch paper up and ask the question
What's important to us about our relationship?
Throw the paper into the bowl and take it in turns to answer the question

Scrunch paper up and ask the question
What do we want more of in this relationship?
Throw the paper into the bowl and take it in turns to answer the question

Scrunch paper up and ask the question
What advantages are there (if any) to each of us in not trying to
make our relationship better?
Throw the paper into the bowl and take it in turns to answer
the question

Scrunch paper up and ask the question
What could we do to stop rowing within this relationship?
Throw the paper into the bowl and take it in turns to answer
the question

Scrunch paper up and ask the question
What will our relationship feel like when we've done that?
Throw the paper into the bowl and take it in turns to answer
the question

'You need chaos
in your soul
to give birth to
a dancing star.'

Friedrich Nietzsche

Our Emotions Diary

Every day this week, notice the emotional atmosphere around you both and talk about it. Are you attracted, fighting, ignoring each other, loving etc? You may find you love each other more than you think. If you don't, it might be time to do something about it. Start by working on the exercises in this chapter.

Underneath your name, write your emotions for each day.

Monday

Partner ....

....

....

....

Date ....

Partner ....

....

....

....

Tuesday

Partner ....

....

....

....

Partner ....

....

....

....

Wednesday

Partner ....

....

....

....

Partner ....

....

....

....

Thursday

Partner ....

....

....

Partner ....

....

....

Friday

Partner ....

....

....

Partner ....

....

....

Saturday

Partner ....

....

....

Partner ....

....

....

Sunday

Partner ....

....

....

Partner ....

....

....

'It is tact that
is golden,
not silence.'

Samuel Butler

Silence Is Not Always Golden

Some relationships disintegrate into silent wars of attrition. Over time you can stop turning towards each other and become increasingly distant and remote until you'd do almost anything rather than communicate. Perhaps one of you digs your heels in. One or both of you may become passive aggressive. Or one partner could be very verbal and have enormous emotional outbursts making the other feel overwhelmed and causing them to shut down. This, in turn, can make the loquacious partner even angrier. Silence can speak volumes.

Sometimes we don't understand why a relationship which was once close feels as if it's drifting apart. The reasons for this may not be the result of a specific episode; it may be that your partner feels that they cannot deal with certain patterns of behaviour and so closes down their channels of communication. Maybe they're hoping that if they ignore the situation it will go away. But it won't go away – it will just get worse.

Patrick and Emma were the envy of all their friends. A glamorous couple, they regularly gave parties at which there was always a sprinkling of celebrities. But when they were on their own things were different. In fact they tried not to be on their own. The only way they could cope with each other was to have other people around who they could interact through. When Patrick came to Life Clubs he told us that the odd times they were together – particularly the times between coming home from work and going out again – Emma would flop in an armchair with a thick stack of papers. She would read for hours just to avoid talking to him. They are now divorced.

This can happen so easily in a relationship. You don't even have to hide behind the papers – simply avoiding eye contact with your partner will stop you bonding. Perhaps your escape route is to get drunk or stoned, have affairs, take up a hobby, work all the time, go obsessively to the gym or make looking after the children take up every available minute of your time. All these will ensure you avoid each other – but at what cost? Whatever form of escape you use, you are not helping yourself or your relationship. You are simply trying to relieve the relationship pain you have. To solve the problem you need to confront it – have those conversations that you have been trying to avoid.

On the following page are some questions for you to think about. If you can, discuss these avoidance techniques together and thank each other for being so open. Maybe your partner got it wrong. Maybe it's not avoidance and you genuinely want to play in the orchestra twice a week. But, maybe they got it right. Either way, acknowledge them and see it from their point of view. 'Thanks for sharing that with me. I can see that it might look as if I don't want to be with you and prefer playing my cello. I'm not sure that's how I do feel.' Then, think about it. What might the cello be replacing in your relationship? Is it easier to join the orchestra than say you're 'too tired for sex'?

A Catch 22 situation

Part of the reason you and your partner are drifting apart may be boredom, but it may also be a feeling of not being secure enough to progress in your relationship. In order to change and start doing things together again, you have to feel safe with your partner, and yet that may only be able to happen once you've made the first change. To create change you can't just get rid of an old habit (avoiding your partner), it's essential to replace it with a new one (refind your enthusiasm for spending time with them). You have to trust things are going to be alright once you've made the first step of being with them again. You may avoid sex, for example, because you don't feel emotionally close, but if you had sex the emotional closeness might come. You have to go for the sex and trust. Take it slowly and step by step over time. Just keep moving forwards.

I Don't Want To Be With You

Read Silence Is Not Always Golden (pages 185-6) before asking yourself
these questions.

Partner ....

What do I do that stops us spending time with each other?
(Think of all the times that you're alone or with others)

Which of these things do I have to do alone and which ones am I doing alone to avoid making contact?

How do I think my partner avoids being with me?

Which of these things will be easy to change and which difficult to change?

Which of my avoidance techniques could I stop using first?

When could I stop using it?

Complete this sentence
'I'd like to spend more time on our relationship. From now on, I'll ...'
(eg '... try to meet my partner for lunch once a week.')

I Don't Want To Be With You/2

Partner ....

What do I do that stops us spending time with each other?
(Think of all the times that you're alone or with others)

....

Which of these things do I have to do alone and which ones am I doing alone to avoid making contact?

....

How do I think my partner avoids being with me?

....

Which of these things will be easy to change and which difficult to change?

....

Which of my avoidance techniques could I stop using first?

....

When could I stop using it?

....

Complete this sentence
'I'd like to spend more time on our relationship. From now on, I'll ...'
(eg '... try to meet my partner for lunch once a week.')

....

....

All Change

At each stage in our lives there are changes. And we have seen that there are crisis times in every relationship. Some changes are natural, some we create ourselves and some other people create for us. Think about what transitions you've been through recently and what's been significant about each of them. Changes impact on us more than we sometimes realise, so stay aware of them and let yourself off the hook a little.

Sometimes, in order to move forward in our relationship, we have to create change. This can be via our attitude, via change in our routine or in something else. These positive changes may require us to compromise or adapt; we might access a part of ourselves we have been fearful of – as Shaun and Niki did.

Shaun and Niki were opposites. He wanted and liked affection; she felt oppressed by his clinginess. Niki loved freedom and was afraid of being trapped. Shaun was afraid of being left. Over the months they worked on changing these behaviour patterns. Shaun began to feel confident of his relationship with Niki and gradually let her go. He no longer felt he needed to be close to her all the time and, because Niki was then free to make up her own mind about the degree of affection she showed Shaun, she slowly turned towards him and began holding his hand and smiling at him. By becoming aware of what the other wanted, and going towards providing it, they deepened their relationship.

Difficulties can arise when one partner changes, because then everything has to change. A partner could be having a baby or approaching retirement or having an affair. These events won't always lead to crisis, but sometimes they can. You have to understand your new story, and you may want to give yourselves time to grieve the old departed one.

When Harry lost a lot of weight, his and Jenny's relationship changed. They'd both been a little on the heavy side and suddenly Jenny didn't know whether she too should change and lose weight, or whether she should just stay as she was and feel guilty. Either way she felt let down. Jenny and

who are we now?

Harry suddenly had different lifestyles. Of course, change can be exciting. In this case Harry's personal growth and physical shrinkage provided an opportunity for their whole relationship to change too. Although Jenny didn't diet, they both started eating differently and their new body shapes gave them renewed confidence. Mealtimes stopped being their focus of attention and instead they started doing more physical things together – including having sex.

Sometimes we become upset because changes don't happen. You may find that when you're feeling sad and cross, it's because a dream you have isn't working out and you're disappointed. It can be a very simple disappointment: 'There was no dancing at the party – I was looking forward to it.' Or it can be a larger disappointment: 'When we met, I imagined you'd become very successful and we'd have a large family'.

What is that dream? What is so important about that dream? Could you accomplish it in a different way? When we blame our partners for our disappointments, it may be that we're actually letting ourselves down. Let your old dreams go and make space for new ones. Enjoy who you are now, together.

Reinvention

When something in your relationship changes, like Harry losing weight, take stock of where you are in your history as a couple. A change has to be acknowledged, respected, and thought about. You can't just pretend it hasn't happened. This is a good time to check together what's happening now.

Answer these questions together :
- **What is the change we are facing now in our relationship?**
- **How did it used to be?**
- **What will we miss about life as it was before?**
- **What is our new history?**
- **What can we keep and bring with us into our new history?**
- **What can we do now that we couldn't do before?**

Design your new history together.

'We do not succeed in changing things according to our desire, but gradually our desire changes.'

Marcel Proust

Relationship Ghosts

It's normal to have unspoken things that 'haunt' your relationship, but it's best to acknowledge them so that they can take a back seat. They can be positive or negative; they're just things that hang between you, and you can feel intuitively even if no-one talks about them. These can be memories of ex-lovers or parents-in-law or of unresolved past rows. When you notice them, bring them out into the open so they can be laid to rest. Decide how you as a couple want to sort them out.

Tim and Maggie had had great sex when Maggie was pregnant. Somehow being pregnant freed Maggie and her exuberance passed itself on to Tim. They enjoyed themselves. Once their first baby was born, however, Maggie didn't feel like having sex at all. She was in pain; the stitches seemed to take forever to heal and she felt distant from Tim emotionally, giving more of her attention to the new baby. Tim realised how Maggie was feeling and left her alone for several months, but one day he started talking about how he missed the sexual adventures they had when Maggie was pregnant. Maggie agreed, she too felt the fun they had once had hanging over them, and it made her feel bad that she didn't feel like that at the moment. That night they made love for the first time since the baby was born – warm, passionate, slow love. Their ghost was out in the open.

Living In Harmony

Who wants to fight continuously? The odd row may be fun, and you can kiss and make up after it, but repeated arguing is no good for any partnership. Think about other places rows occur in your life – at work or with family? What can you learn from those disagreements? Here are four ways to calm your rows down. Remember that neither of you has to be 'right' – there are many ways to look at any issue.

Four ways to have a calmer row

1. Start gently and with humour.
- **Pick your moment. A lot of women swear that after sex is a great time to levy a little complaint – others say it's the worst possible time. In front of the children or other bystanders is never good**
- **Start by how you are feeling, 'I'm upset because …'**
- **Describe what's happening without being judgemental. 'I feel like I'm the only one who is planning our holiday and I'd appreciate your help.' Remember the tone is as important as the words you use**
- **Be clear about what you want 'I'd like it if …'**
- **Be polite: 'Please can you help me organise the children's party today?'**
- **Be appreciative: 'It was such fun when you used to take me out to the cinema'**
- **Don't store things up – keep talking**

2. Keep calm
- **Ask your partner to help you calm down if you feel out of control**
- **Tell your partner you want to be on your own for a bit to collect yourself**
- **Take time out and listen to music, exercise, meditate, read – take twenty minutes apart**

finding common ground

3. Be willing to reach out at any time and allow your partner to do the same

- Aim to stop the fight as early as possible: 'Can we stop rowing please? I'm not enjoying this.' But acknowledge there's still an issue to sort out
- Admit you're wrong
- Apologise – remove the tension
- Pull a face, be silly, make both of you laugh
- Rather than hurl criticisms: 'You are so pigheaded', 'Why do you never listen to what I am saying?' express your feelings: 'I feel worried … Scared … unhappy … Criticised'
- Get to 'Yes' as quickly as possible: 'I understand what you're saying.' 'Please can we stop this? It doesn't seem to be getting anywhere except making me feel sad'
- Understand that your partner loves you and wants to please you
- Remember this old German saying – 'The wiser one gives in'

4. Find common ground between the two of you

- Treat your partner as you would a friend – be tolerant, hold on to your manners and dignity. Accept them as they are
- Get in touch with your needs and ask your partner how you can meet their needs
- Be open to their ideas
- Compromise
- Try to become a team again

'In the middle of
every difficulty
lies opportunity.'

Albert Einstein

Perspectives

Often, when arguing, we say things that we really didn't mean. You can never take them back, but you can explain to your partner that they weren't accurate and that you wish you hadn't said them. If you have to row it's crucial that afterwards you can repair the damage you've caused to each other. Once you're calm, start talking. Acknowledge the problem and discuss it as much as you can without anger or blame. Hold on to your humour and don't get overwhelmed. Think about how it could be different next time. Be honest with your partner; use, 'I feel ...', 'I want ...' when talking to them. Ask them what they want to ask you. Remember there is no 'right' answer. No-one is ever 'right'.

The more perspectives you can bring to any issue, the greater the possibility of finding a solution. It's as if you are presenting lots of 'truths' to the problem. The problem ceases to have one 'truth' that has to be found – suddenly there is a choice from which to choose a compromise.

Which perspective?

We all become wedded to our own solutions. If our chosen solution doesn't work out, instead of dropping it, we may blame someone else or just keep trying the same solution with greater intensity; we sometimes just end up saying the same thing louder and louder, like the caricature tourist on holiday trying to be understood. That's the way we can be when we want to get our point of view across – and it doesn't work.

Thinking of different perspectives will shift your focus out of an existing outlook, and open up new points of view. New perspectives provide new information, make you think thoughts that were previously unthinkable and help you look at your situation from another angle. Sometimes even just shifting your position around the room a little bit as you are arguing can be the first perspective change.

Changing Perspective
Think about these very simple perspective shifts

Partner ....

What's my take on this particular issue?

....

....

What would my favourite cartoon character think about this particular issue?

....

....

What might my mother say if I asked her advice?

....

....

And what would my favourite TV/film character say?

....

....

Get the idea?

Changing Perspective/2

Partner ....

What's my take on this particular issue?

....

....

What would my favourite cartoon character think about this particular issue?

....

....

What might my mother say if I asked her advice?

....

....

And what would my favourite TV/film character say?

....

....

Get the idea?

Rocky Us is all about ...   understanding that conflict is natural
realising what can trigger rows
moving forward in our quest to stop rowing
becoming a team and solving the
    problem together
finding out how we feel about each other
avoiding avoidance
working with change
outing ghosts
building bridges
seeing things from different perspectives

finding my future

8

future us

The Circle Of Life

As we approach the end of the book, it's time to start thinking about what you want for the future. No doubt you sometimes feel that life would be simpler if it was just the two of you alone in isolation enjoying each other. But it's hardly ever like that – we're usually part of a complex network. We maybe someone's mum or dad, someone's colleague, someone's friend, someone's son or daughter.

The Circle of Life is a starting point for seeing who (and what) makes up everything else in your life, and for understanding what changes you want to make. It's about externalising your emotions and solving your problems in a very simple visual way. It will help you to see how current problems are often linked to other people and interests in your life – as well as just the two of you. You can use the Circle of Life to access your feelings and to express to your partner what you're going through. It's both fun and illuminating. Don't think too much, just draw away.

Making a Circle of Life

1. Start by drawing a big circle – or use the ones on the following pages. That circle represents your life. You can now choose a problem to work through or simply think about your life at present

2. Next draw yourself as a smaller circle inside the big circle. This circle can be whatever size you want and you can put yourself anywhere in the larger circle

3. Then draw some further circles inside or outside the large circle. Each circle you now draw represents one of the people important to you in your life: a member of your family, a friend, an enemy, a neighbour, a colleague – whoever you like. Put as many of them into your Circle of Life as you want to. Place these circles wherever you want and draw them large or small, overlapping or not. The larger they are, the more important they are, and the position you put them in shows how you see them in relation to you. If you put them near you, they're important to you and if they're far away from you, they're not as important. You can even put them outside the big circle. Be totally honest about where you want to put each circle and what size you want

'When a finger points
to the moon the fool
looks at the finger.'

Chinese proverb

to make it. This circle is a visual representation of the way you
see your life as it is now

4. **Then put in all the other important areas of your life – your
religion, work, hobbies, pets etc. Draw them in as circles too –
again as large or small as you want to and as near or far away
from you as you wish**
5. **If you are having an argument or row or are ill or unhappy, put a
circle for that in as well**
6. **As you go along, write in each circle who or what it stands for**

*Alison had had a huge row with her girl friends and felt ostracised. She'd
just moved home to be nearer to them and this was the worst thing that
could have happened. To add to her woes, she'd broken up with her
boyfriend. She felt totally alone and as if she had no-one to talk to. When
Alison drew her Circle of Life, she could plainly see that she only really had
her family to talk to; her friends were all clustered together at the far side of
the circle – as far away from her as they could be. When Alison then drew
her future Circle of Life – representing what she would like her life to be
like next year – her friends were all back surrounding her, but they were all
overlapping each other and at a slight distance from Alison. When we
talked about what was stopping them from overlapping her too, Alison
started to think about the way she conducted her relationships. She realised
that she kept everyone she loved at arm's length to protect herself. Alison
could see that the fact she never really let her friends come close to her and
was never totally relaxed with them might be the reason why they were
deserting her now.*

Another, more organic, way of playing this game is to use found objects,
such as shells, pebbles, buttons etc. on sand or pavement or wherever
you can draw a big circle. Objects come in different shapes, sizes and
colours, and can easily be moved around on the paper; it becomes clear
to see that if you move one piece you may well have to move some of
the others. For example, once Alison had moved her friends closer to
her, she would have had to think about her relationship with her family
and how that would change. You can also think about, and express, why

you chose that particular pebble to represent that particular person or thing or state of mind.

Start by plotting your partner's Circle of Life
Imagine the Circle of Life your partner would draw – and draw it yourself. (And vice versa – get them to imagine yours.) Look at your version and their circle side by side – what do they tell you? What assumptions have you made about your partner's feelings, about the people and things in their life? Those assumptions will be just as revealing as the way your partner draws their own circle. Both will give you food for thought.

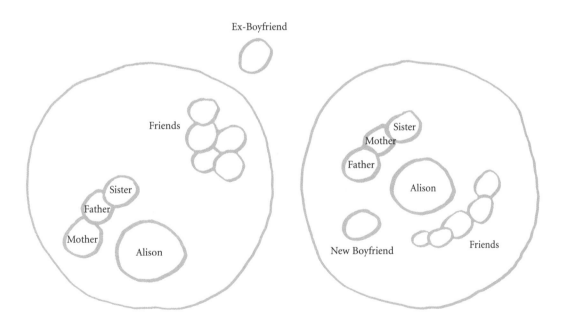

Alison's present Circle of Life   **Alison's future Circle of Life**

My Partner's Circle Of Life

Partner .... **Date** ....

Start by drawing a Circle of Life for your partner. What do you imagine
their circle would look like? Cover this circle with a piece of paper
before your partner draws theirs opposite.

My Circle Of Life

Partner ....   **Date** ....

Before you look at the assumptions your partner made about your
Circle of Life on the opposite page, draw your own Circle of Life here.
Then discuss both circles, what the differences are and what makes you
each think the way you do.

My Partner's Circle Of Life

Partner ....   **Date** ....

Start by drawing a Circle of Life for your partner. What do you imagine
their circle would look like? Cover this circle with a piece of paper
before your partner draws theirs opposite

My Circle Of Life

Partner ....   **Date** ....

Before you look at the assumptions your partner made about your
Circle of Life on the opposite page, draw your own Circle of Life here.
Then discuss both circles, what the differences are and what makes you
each think the way you do.

Talking about the Circle of Life

The Circle of Life need only take a few minutes to plot out, but it can be interesting to spend a little time thinking about what you've created and why. Once you have compared your circle with the one your partner drew up for you, continue to tell the story of your Circle of Life focusing on each circle or object and explaining its relationship to the other circles/objects. There is no right or wrong – you are just explaining the way you see your life as it is now.

Here are some questions to ask yourself – or that your partner could ask you – and you can both make up your own:

- **Do I like the picture I've created?**
- **Is there anything that I feel is unexpected?**
- **What would I like to change in this picture and therefore in my life?**
- **Why are some of the circles bigger or smaller than others?**
- **Why are some of the circles overlapping when others aren't?**
- **What's relevant about the differing spaces between them?**
- **Why are some circles outside the big circle?**
- **How do my work/interests affect various relationships?**
- **If we could shrink the problem/unhappiness in this or that area, would any of the circles move or grow?**

Future Circle of Life

You can now draw another circle and work out how you would like your life to be in a year's time. What do you want to change? Think of one step you could take towards creating your new system. When could you take it? How will you feel when you've done it? Work towards your ideal scenario, both on your own and as a couple.

Again, it can be easier to visualise your future using found objects. Discuss each change you make. For example, 'If we took away this big red button, which is your work, and changed it to a small, blue button, how does life look for you?' or, 'What about if you moved this button (your bossy sister) from the middle to the side, what would your life look like?' or, 'If this relationship (with my mother – the little green button) changed, what would happen to our relationship?

My Future Circle Of Life

Partner ....   Date ....

What do you want your circle to be like in a year's time? Fantasise about it and imagine what it could be. Now think about the changes you'll have to make to get it like that.

Here are some examples of questions to think about while you are drawing your future circle of life, or you can make up your own:

- **If work takes up less time than it does now, what will fill the space that it leaves?**
- **If my children leave home, or we have a child, how will the circles change?**
- **Do we have space in our future circles to take up new hobbies?**

creating our future

'Come out of
the circle of time
And into the
circle of love.'

Rumi

My Future Circle Of Life

Partner ....   **Date** ....

What do you want your circle to be like in a year's time? Fantasise about it and imagine what it could be. Now think about the changes you'll have to make to get it like that.

Here are some examples of questions to think about while you are drawing your future circle of life, or you can make up your own:

- If work takes up less time than it does now, what will fill the space that it leaves?
- If my children leave home, or we have a child, how will the circles change?
- Do we have space in our future circles to take up new hobbies?

Our Circle Of Life

Work together on a Circle of Life involving everyone in both your lives.
This is your chance to think about what you have now and what you
want for your future together.

I'll Tell You What I Want

We're often not good at asking for what we want. We may feel it's embarrassing or maybe we feel that our partners should already know – they should be able to read our minds in the same way it appeared as if our parents or early carers could. But we've become more sophisticated in our demands – we no longer just want some milk or our favourite toy brought to us – and often our partners don't know what we'd like. Rather than feeling let down and angry if your partner doesn't give you what you want, tell them.

This is a chance to let your partner know what you really want from them. Tell them, and then listen to what they want from you. Take it in turns to write down what you want. If these things then start happening to you, make sure you tell your partner that you appreciate them happening.

I Love It

Partner ....

What you do that makes me feel loved …
(eg when you ask me questions about my childhood, give me compliments)

....

....

What you used to do that made me feel loved …
(eg when you blew down the back of my neck, brought me a cup of
tea in bed)

....

....

I would feel loved if you …
(eg took me away for the weekend, taught me how to play tennis)

....

....

'My bounty is as boundless as the sea, My love as deep; the more I give to thee, The more I have, for both are infinite.'

William Shakespeare

I Love It/2

Partner ....

What you do that makes me feel loved ...
(eg when you ask me questions about my childhood, give me compliments)

....

....

....

What you used to do that made me feel loved ...
(eg when you blew down the back of my neck, brought me a cup of
tea in bed)

....

....

....

I would feel loved if you ...
(eg took me away for the weekend, taught me how to play tennis)

....

....

....

I'll Tell You What I Like

Before thinking about the future, ground yourselves in the present. Get cosy together – light a fire, sit where you can see the sunset. Feel a glow. Remind yourselves what you like about each other now. See if you can fill the answers in at the same time without ripping the book in half – you may have to snuggle up close to do it.

Partner ....

What three things do we like doing together?

1.
2.
3.

What three things do we like about each other?

1.
2.
3.

What three things do we like doing to each other?

1.
2.
3.

What three things do I like you doing to me?

1.
2.
3.

Which one shall we do now?

I'll Tell You What I Like/2

Partner ....

What three things do we like doing together?

1.
2.
3.

What three things do we like about each other?

1.
2.
3.

What three things do we like doing to each other?

1.
2.
3.

What three things do I like you doing to me?

1.
2.
3.

Which one shall we do now?

'Life is the flower
for which love is
the honey.' **Victor Hugo**

Create Your Own History

Closeness comes not only from sharing a present and a future, but also a past. You've already got a past together, but it's a great idea to consolidate your own myths about your relationship and formalise any traditions you have already created.

Happy memories are a happy future

Begin with your history – a history that doesn't need reinventing, but strengthening. Write down everything you can remember about your relationship, from the first time you clapped eyes on each other to today. Include your first meeting, your first date, your first kiss, your first holiday, the first time you met each other's parents, and so on.

This is the time to bring out old photos of the two of you. Create a collage of past times and frame it.

What Do We Remember About ...

	What happened	Date
When we first met		
Our first date		
Our first kiss		
Any special kisses		
Special music we listened to		
Other early dates		
Our first Valentine's day		
Parties we went to		
Early sex		
Our first presents		
Other presents		
Our first holiday		
Other holidays		
Any special sex		

	What happened	Date
Happiest times		
Worst times		
Most embarrassing times		
First party we gave		
Our first home		
Meeting each other's parents		
Meeting each other's friends		
Meeting each other's relations		
First baby		
Subsequent children		
Any other memories		

'God gave
us memories
that we might
have roses
in December.'

J.M. Barrie

Our Rituals

It's important for you as a couple to keep your shared history fresh. Traditions and rituals are shared experiences and are good for a relationship. They create a firm foundation to build on, and fall back on when times seem a bit rocky.

Most of us have three types of rituals: the type that springs from our religion or culture, family traditions that link us to our parents and grandparents and routines and rituals that have evolved organically. Within our relationship, these first two types of rituals can cause disagreements – this is why it's particularly important to evolve your own shared history. You can create your own rituals around holidays, celebrations, everyday greetings, illness, weekends, bedtime routines, dates, meals, entertaining, sex, children, goodbyes, time alone – anything. They will determine your common identity and shared beliefs.

Martin and Alison were particularly competitive as a couple. They used endlessly to challenge each other about everything and anything and would often bet each other a pound about something. They put this pound in a little heart box and it went back and forwards between them depending on who was right. This pound became a ritual between the two of them – it was a shared joke about how they both had to be right. This ritual made their competitiveness constructive. One day an artist friend of theirs came for the weekend and captured the pound and the box in a painting. Their ritual had been immortalised.

Rituals will bind you together as a couple and, later, as a family.

What's Important To Us

You're creating a history of yourselves as a couple. It's time to begin designing the relationship you want now and in the future. Think about yourselves together as you answer these five questions.

1. When friends call us a 'great couple' what do we think they mean?

....

....

2. What brings us happiness as a couple?

....

....

3. How do we want our relationship to feel?

....

....

4. What will we commit to for each other?

....

....

5. What do we want more of?

....

....

....

Creating Our Future

Happy couples help each other realise their dreams. You can support each other in achieving them by becoming a part of each other's dreams, helping the other financially and emotionally.

Start with a fantasy

Can you project yourself into the future and imagine looking back on this time in your life? Suppose you were to imagine the two of you in five, or even ten years' time, where would you be and what would you be doing? What would you be saying about this time in your relationship? How would you like to be getting on? What would you like to be most proud of regarding your relationship?

There are usually things you haven't yet done – fantasies that you might like to fulfil. If you could have one of those dreams come true, what would it be for each of you?

My dream (Partner ....)

....

....

My dream (Partner ....)

....

....

Imagine achieving that dream

- **What is the essence of that dream?**
- **What is it about that dream that feels so good?**
- **How else could you achieve that same feeling?**
- **What would the fulfilment of your dream mean to others?**

'If you have built castles in the air, your work need not be lost; that is where they should be. Now put the foundations under them.' Henry David Thoreau

Your Balance Chart

You're almost at the end of this book now. You've been through an enormous journey together and have stretched and grown. You've filled in the Balance Chart as a couple once before, now it's time to fill it in again, but this time with all the new ideas you have about yourselves and your relationship. It's exciting. See how much you've changed since you started this book, how much bigger your dreams have become.

Go round the Balance Chart together for the final time, making shared goals and writing down what you want from each segment in the present tense. Be positive (eg we have fun together and respect each other, we have a large, happy family, we are both working in a career we enjoy). Then mark on the Balance Chart how close to that goal you think you are. '10' is for very close, '1' for not very close. What could you do to work towards your '10'?

What are our goals in the Love and Romance section?

What are our goals in the Home section?

What are our goals in the Family section?

What are our goals in the Creativity section?

What are our goals in the Health and Fitness section?

What are our goals in the Rest and Relaxation section?

What are our goals in the Friends and Social Life section?

What are our goals in the Career section?

What are our goals in the Money section?

What are our goals in the Spirituality section?

filling in our future

Our Future Balance Chart

Today's date ....

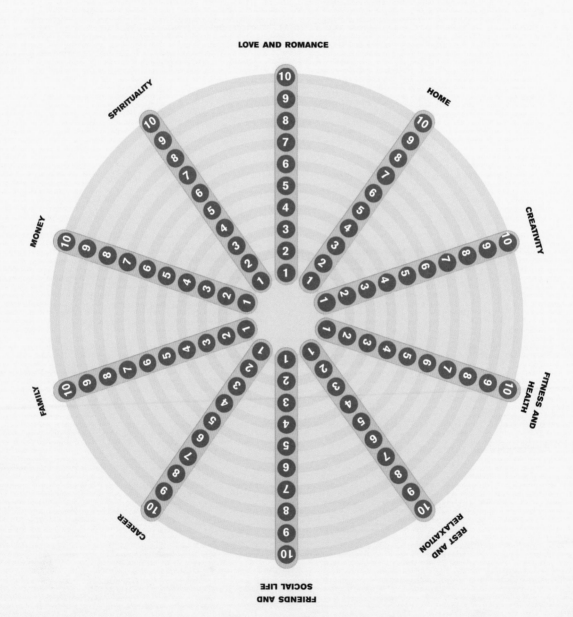

Future Us is all about ...   visualising ourselves and our relationships today
visualising ourselves in the future
sharing what we love about each other
creating a shared history together
understanding what we want from our relationship
thinking about our dreams
working out our Balance Chart together

what next?

What Next?

You have finished this book and started the wonderful process of having conscious relationships, of being aware that there is always more to discover about you and your partner. No matter what stage of your relationship you are at, enjoy seeing every day as a beginning and your relationship will continue to unfold.

You change daily, as do both your partner and your relationship. That means it's always time to start re-examining who you both are, so that you can get the most out of each other. It's an ongoing process and it never tires.

Becoming conscious of yourself, your partner and your relationship is exciting. Seeing someone you've known for a long time afresh is eye-opening. Often our romantic times and our arguments become habit and routine. Each row seems less urgent, but so does each affirmation of love – if they happen at all. It can be good not to have passionate arguments, to be in a calmer state of commitment, but not if it's a habit rather than a conscious choice. A relationship needs to be lived consciously or it will die.

Often when we run away from relationships, we are attempting to run away from ourselves, to avoid facing everything that isn't perfect about us. We try to stop ourselves getting depressed by constantly chasing romance or something new with others, rather than looking for romance within ourselves. Being in a relationship involves facing, and being seen with, our downs as well as our ups – our dark as well as our bright sides. Once we can trust ourselves and our partners, and begin to be honest within the relationship, we are on our way to a true commitment.

True commitment happens when we stop trying to change ourselves or our partners to make them fit into our expectations of what a relationship ought to be like. It happens when we just relax and enjoy what is, when we accept that changes happen between two people and when we trust that these changes will be positive for both of us. When we don't blame each other for how things are, but realise that both of us are responsible for the relationship. When we treat each other as we would treat our friends.

Part of the joy of commitment is when you can both see that there are more perspectives than just 'my way' or 'your way' of doing and thinking things – when you can create an 'our way', a compromise that you've enjoyed creating consciously together. You don't always have to agree as a couple, you just have to share both the bad and the good and express what each of you feels. With each problem you share you create new ways of solving it within the relationship. Becoming intimate involves revealing more and more of yourself to another – risking comfort for honesty. Truly being yourself helps to make relationships really fulfilling and creative. Feeling nervous? You've got nothing to lose.

Commit to discovery, commit to exploration, keep talking, keep questioning, keep listening. But most of all enjoy everything about yourself and each other.

Nina Grunfeld, October 2006

life clubs

Life Clubs

What exactly is a Life Club?

Life Clubs are once-a-week workshops. At each Club you are given not only practical tools to help you understand yourself and move your life forward, but also constant encouragement. At Life Clubs we inspire you step by step to fulfil your potential and realise your dreams.

To date we've got eighteen clubs around the country and, hopefully, by the time this book appears in the shops, we'll have around thirty reaching from Edinburgh to Chichester.

I created Life Clubs to echo the experiences I had in my teens and twenties when I used to hitch-hike. It was always fascinating and liberating to talk to the person who drove you in a truly open and honest way. You knew they held no secret agenda for you. Life Clubs is like this. It's different – and freeing.

Life Clubs are helping others to change their lives and discover more about themselves and they're doing things they never dreamt were possible. We've had Life Clubs clients writing plays, setting up their own companies and even emigrating. They've found happiness.

I too have found happiness. I've started living the life I've always wanted to live – running my own business with a family of colleagues supporting me – envisioning a future that seems to be coming true every moment. People are reaching out to me in the same way I'm reaching out to them, and that's a great feeling.

What about the future?

My vision is big. I'd like to have Life Clubs all around the country so you could all experience one. Why not come and join us?

Nina Grunfeld

These are some of the things people have said about Life Clubs

'I think Life Clubs are great. I come away feeling positive and encouraged by the success stories of others. I will go again and encourage others to as well.' **Kathleen**

'Feel I have changed, something magic has happened, I feel happier and more accepting of my life here.' **Asylum seeker from Iraq**

'I've made major changes and it's started with little things. There's always an excuse to stop getting a life. With Life Clubs I realised I was the brick wall. It's good to drop in and out of. It keeps you on your toes.' **Mary Lou**

'Life Clubs are great as I don't feel judged and I feel supported. I can make plans for the following week that are indiviual to me and needn't worry that I don't meet other people's expectations.' **Howard**

'I totally believe Life Clubs gave me the extra motivation and encouragement to get my life in better balance and put into practice goal-setting strategies.' **Kate**

'Coming on the Mondays has enabled me to focus more on life, my goals and achievements and has helped me to grow more as a person, as well as enabling me to interact with some wonderful people.' **David**

'I really enjoyed yesterday's meeting. Thank you! It was really insightful and just the fact that I chose to do something for myself by myself was absolutely awesome.' **Barbara**

'I'm having a lot of fun learning about how to get where I want to be' **Hilary**

'To be trusted is a greater compliment than to be loved.'

George MacDonald

Acknowledgments

I want to thank everyone who has trusted me. I cannot tell them how much it's meant.

Starting from the top
Henry Morris

Those who I really can't thank enough, who've trusted me implicitly
Maurits Kalff, Annie Lionnet, Janie Romer, Lucy Sisman, Nicholas Underhill and our children (Michael, Frances, Ursula and Tommy), Jane Whistler, Gill and Robin Yourston

Coaches who have stuck with me from the start (in the order I met them) Annie Lionnet, Gordon Melvin, Philippa Heseltine, Mia Forbes-Pirie, Rachel Bamber, Anya Hubrath

Other Coaches - past, present and future
Rosslyn Albright, Shamash Alidina, Helen Baker, Penny Beard, Julia Brightwell, Duncan Brodie, Samantha Brook, Mandy Bruce, Stewart Burlison, Paul Burton, Christine Chalkin, Dawn Chalmers, Julia Collett, Beatriz de Luis Casquero, Joanna Desborough-Brown, Caroline Doughty, Andrew Farrow, Helen Gerlach, Sidsel Giaever, Una Goulding, Paul Graber, Samantha Grainger, Sarah Harrison, Lesley Hepburn, Jonathan Hill, Lynne Irwin, Nina Johnson, Charlotte Jones, Moira Kettle, Priscillia Joseph, Kim Kelly, Debbie Legerton, Mark Lister, Michael MacMahon, James Marshall, Bob Merckel, Yvonne Morecroft, Tony Phillips, Emma Player, Susie Pratt, Christin Rauter, Julia Robson, Janie Romer, Sohan Singh, Susan Swift, Jackie Thoms, Cyndy Walker, Annabel Weeden

Thanks so much for either starting a local Life Club or working with Corporate Life Clubs.

Life Clubs Clients

I also wanted to thank all the forward-thinking clients who have come to Life Clubs. We've really enjoyed getting to know you.

Wordsmiths

Julia Booth-Clibborn, Sally Marlow, Gordon Melvin (for his eloquent Balance Chart description), Hugo Stanley, Nicholas Underhill

Designers

Cecilia Carey, David Eldridge and everyone at Two Associates (for two stunning looking books), Dan Price (for great stationery, hands-on website creation and overall design help), Lucy Sisman (for two incredible logos and websites)

Those who've helped and advised me

Geoffrey Bayliss, Matthew Durdy, Charles Elton, Andrew Gifford, Georgia Grunfeld, Gitta Grunfeld, Mandy Grunfeld, Micky Johnson, Irene Samuels, Tom Underhill

Those who worked with me on a day-to-day basis

Alice Carey, Katalin Szecsodi, Thorsten Zerha

Daily Telegraph team

Casilda Grigg, Cassandra Jardine, Stuart Penney and Jon Stock

Short Books team

Special thanks to Aurea Carpenter and Rebecca Nicolson and thanks also to their team – Emily Fox (for all her insights), Catherine Gibbs, Angela Martin and Vanessa Webb

Capel & Land

Georgina Capel and Abi Fellows

For turning me on to the Enneagram personality typing system

Paul and Rosemary Cowan, Gordon Melvin and Jane Whistler